One Soldier's Story

WWII Service Record: Leyte & Okinawa

Jacob Wesley Zimmerli

Edited by Michael Zimmerli

Additional Interview Material Courtesy of Adam Zimmerli

Notice of Copyright

Copyright © 2021 Michael Zimmerli. All rights reserved.

The characters and events portrayed in this book are real. This is a first-hand memoir of historical events and the people involved.

No part of this book may be reproduced, or stored in a retrieval system, or transmitted in any form or by any means, electronic, mechanical, photocopying, recording, or otherwise, without express written permission of the publisher. For permission, email mike@zimmac.com

Cover Design & Edited By: Michael Zimmerli

First Printing, 2021

Author information updated 2024 to reflect the author's passing.

DEDICATION

This book is dedicated to the members of the 96th Infantry Division, the Deadeyes. To the men I fought with and worked with and will never forget.

—Jacob Wesley Zimmerli

CONTENTS

SPECIAL THANKS

I owe special thanks to my son, Adam Zimmerli, for the use of his interview with his grandfather in March of 2004. The interview provided extra comments and insight from Wes as he and Adam went through the information. The transcript of that interview provided much of the extra information for this book.

Wes had originally recorded his memoirs of his WWII Service in preparation for the interview with Adam. That interview was for Adam's senior college project: to interview a veteran of the Pacific Theater from WWII. Those interviews were placed in the National Archives.

Growing up as one of Wes's five sons, I knew he had been in WWII, but it was something he didn't talk about. Mom said he only talked about it with others who had been there with him, on those rare occasions when he could attend a Deadeyes reunion. That's why it was surprising when he began opening up about his service time after he retired in 1989.

I remember one time when Adam asked him to come to his school – Adam was in high school at the time, I believe – and speak to his history class about his experiences. And Dad did it. And then when Adam was in his senior year at college, his senior project involved interviewing a WWII veteran of the Pacific Theater. I was surprised again to find out Dad was writing down his experiences so he could speak coherently and concisely for the interview. When he was done, I edited his manuscript and we made it available as a pdf on my website and later we added it to others on rememberthedeadeyes.com.

There are approximately 245 WWII veterans dying each day. Many are passing without ever telling anyone their stories and memories from their time in service. This information inspired Wes to agree to the interview and write his memoirs. He feels it is important for the younger generations to have this information to learn from.

In 2020, it was estimated that there were 300,000 veterans of WWII still alive, 75 years after the surrender of Germany in the European Theater and Japan in the Pacific Theater.

This is more than just one soldier's story. These are my dad's memories of that difficult time. He is my soldier, my hero, and this is his story.

—Michael Zimmerli, ed.

JACOB WESLEY ZIMMERLI
US 37 586 226
Sergeant
Company B, 383rd Infantry Regiment
96th "Deadeye" Infantry Division
February 7, 1944 to February 8, 1946

Introduction

The 96th Infantry Division: The Deadeyes

Special to The Oregonian/OregonLive

By Lynne Hasselman

November 10, 2019

(Reprinted by Permission)

Known as the Deadeyes for their marksmanship, the 96th Infantry Division went from an inexperienced division led by regular Oregonians to a courageous and skilled amphibious unit that fought with distinction in two of the most brutal and fabled battles of the Pacific Theater -- Leyte and Okinawa.

The 96th Infantry Division was Oregon's own military unit, activated into combat at Camp Adair north of Corvallis on August 15, 1942. Its men, most draftees from the Pacific Northwest and the Midwest, trained there in addition to the high desert of Central Oregon and Camp White in Medford.

They entered combat on October 20, 1944, on Leyte, a narrow island that Gen. Douglas MacArthur had planned to use as a significant Army Air Corps base.

As the Deadeyes slogged through the water from their landing crafts to the beach, they couldn't imagine the hell that awaited them.

They fought tenaciously through the swamps, rice paddies, jungles, ravines, and mountains. Lt. Robert E. Gaines of Portland and Sgt. John C. Rea of Salem commanded platoons on the front lines, knocking out machine gun nests and fighting with bayonets and trench knives.

During Leyte's monsoon rains, the Deadeyes climbed slippery, muddy slopes to knock out fortified pillboxes with artillery, grenades, and flamethrowers. They grabbed a few hours of rest in foxholes filled with stagnant water and wore the same wet boots until the skin on their feet and ankles sloughed off. They caught dengue fever, malaria, and dysentery.

By the time Leyte was declared secure on Christmas Day 1944, the 96th Infantry Division lost 376 officers and enlisted men, 1,000 more had been wounded, and 2,500 had fallen victim to injury or illness. Those left to carry on were battle-hardened, sick, demoralized, and exhausted.

Yet their hardest test was still to come.

On April 1, 1945, the Deadeyes would meet the Japanese Army's "typhoon of steel" on Okinawa in the bloodiest battle of the Pacific War.

Just after dawn on Okinawa's landing day, which fell on Easter Sunday, the Navy began a pre-invasion bombardment of the island, and carrier planes struck the shore and trenches with napalm. Over a breakfast of steak and eggs, the Deadeyes were tense and somber. Within a few hours, they would come face to face with 155,000 troops ready to fight to the death.

A continuous cloud of black smoke hung over the troopships to protect them against kamikaze attacks, and the acrid sulfur smell of cordite explosives hung in the air. An armada of Landing Ship Tanks circled, waiting to take the troops to the beach. As transport ships played the popular Bing Crosby song, "Easter Parade" over the speakers, the men of the 96th Infantry Division began descending the cargo nets to the landing craft that would take them ashore.

Landing on Okinawa, the men ran onto the sand, yelling fiercely as they stormed the cratered beach. Other than light artillery fire in the distance, there was no resistance.

The enemy fighters were waiting in prepared positions on the ridgelines. The Deadeyes shifted south and took their first heavy casualties at Kakazu Ridge.

The battle of Conical Hill, the six long ridges defended by more than 1,000 Japanese troops, was the most treacherous battle that Staff Sgt. Orrie H. Gruwell from Enterprise, OR ever encountered. Gruwell, a platoon guide, told the "Deadeye Dispatch," the 96th Infantry Division Association's newsletter, that he and his men advanced behind flame-throwing tanks. Firing their machine guns while the ground burned, they attacked until all resistance ceased.

Monsoon rains turned Okinawa into a morass of ankle-deep mud, and foxholes and trenches were filled with water. The hills and ravines were littered with shell casings, mortar shell containers, and abandoned supplies. Corpses of enemy soldiers lay decaying in the mire.

The battle for Okinawa lasted for 82 days. On June 22, 1945, the American flag was raised over the 10th Army Headquarters and the island was declared secure. The 96th Infantry Division lost 1,625 men in action on Okinawa and over 7,500 were wounded.

Some 880 Deadeyes were evacuated from Okinawa due to combat fatigue from what they saw and experienced. Some blocked it out completely. Many never talked about it, even with their families.

The remaining Deadeyes left Okinawa for Mindoro, Philippines, to rest and prepare their next action, this one even more dreaded. They would invade Japan.

The U.S. dropped the nuclear bomb on Hiroshima on August 6, 1945, and on Nagasaki three days later. Six days later, Emperor Hirohito surrendered, and the war was over.

The Deadeyes celebrated with three allotted beers a piece. They were the lucky ones -- they were going home.[1]

---

[1] (Hasselmann 2019)

This is the story of one of those who came home, and after 70 years, told his story. This is One Soldier's Story.

Preface to War

PRESIDENT FRANKLIN D. ROOSEVELT'S MESSAGE ASKING CONGRESS TO DECLARE WAR AGAINST JAPAN AFTER THE ATTACK ON PEARL HARBOR

December 8, 1941

"Yesterday, December 7, 1941 — a date which will live in infamy — the United States of America was suddenly and deliberately attacked by naval and air forces of the Empire of Japan.

The United States was at peace with that Nation and, at the solicitation of Japan, was still in conversation with its Government and its Emperor looking toward the maintenance of peace in the Pacific. Indeed, one hour after Japanese air squadrons had commenced bombing in the American Island of Oahu, the Japanese Ambassador to the United States and his colleague delivered to our Secretary of State a formal reply to a recent American message. And while this reply stated that it seemed useless to continue the existing diplomatic negotiations, it contained no threat or hint of war or armed attack.

It will be recorded that the distance of Hawaii from Japan makes it obvious that the attack was deliberately planned many days or even weeks ago. During the intervening time, the Japanese Government has deliberately sought to deceive the United States by false statements and expressions of hope for continued peace.

The attack yesterday on the Hawaiian Islands has caused severe damage to American naval and military forces. I regret to tell you that very many American lives have been lost. In addition, American ships have been reported torpedoed on the high seas between San Francisco and Honolulu.

Yesterday the Japanese Government also launched an attack against Malaya.

Last night Japanese forces attacked Hong Kong.

Last night Japanese forces attacked Guam.

Last night Japanese forces attacked the Philippine Islands. Last night the Japanese attacked Wake Island. And this morning the Japanese attacked Midway Island.

Japan has, therefore, undertaken a surprise offensive extending throughout the Pacific area. The facts of yesterday and today speak for themselves. The people of the United States have already formed their opinions and well understand the implications to the very life and safety of our Nation.

As Commander in Chief of the Army and Navy, I have directed that all measures be taken for our defense.

But always will our whole Nation remember the character of the onslaught against us.

No matter how long it may take us to overcome this premeditated invasion, the American people, in their righteous might, will win through to absolute victory. I believe that I interpret the will of the Congress and of the people when I assert that we will not only defend ourselves to the uttermost but will make it very certain that this form of treachery shall never again endanger us.

Hostilities exist. There is no blinking at the fact that our people, our territory, and our interests are in grave danger.

With confidence in our armed forces - with the unbounding determination of our people - we will gain the inevitable triumph – so help us God.

I ask that the Congress declare that since the unprovoked and dastardly attack by Japan on Sunday, December 7, 1941, a state of war has existed between the United States and the Japanese Empire."

—Franklin Delano Roosevelt

President, United States of America

[2] The iconic recruiting poster with Uncle Sam.

---

[2] Flagg, James Montgomery, ca. 1917

³ One raw recruit. Just a quick dash home before catching the train to the west coast for basic training. In the Army for less than a week.

---

[3] J. W. Zimmerli, One Raw Recruit 1944. Private collection.

CHAPTER 1

Starting Out

Camp White and Basic Training

I was inducted into the U.S. Army on February 7, 1944, at Ft. Snelling, Minnesota. We were issued our uniforms, given a series of shots, assigned to a barracks, and immediately put to work cleaning the floors. This was supposedly done so that we would not notice how sore our arms were from the series of shots we had just received. It worked!!

The next day, we were assigned to work details. My work detail was in the blood testing room in the facility where we had been inducted. For three days during duty hours, I sterilized needles and kept the medics supplied with needles and other supplies.

Each day we would check the assignment board to see who was being sent to basic training somewhere.

("You were excited, but you didn't know what was going to happen. That was the other side of the coin. You didn't know what you were getting into. And you couldn't back out. You couldn't back out then." - Zimmerli, Jacob W. 15 March 2004 interview with Adam Zimmerli)

Soon, my name showed up on the board, saying I was going to the 96th Infantry Division at Camp White, Oregon. I was informed I could have a pass to go home to visit before shipping out to my new base. I took a Greyhound Bus to Jackson, MN, with Harold Bute, who was also inducted with me and was also going to Camp White.

After reporting back to Ft. Snelling, we boarded a troop train for Oregon. It was my first journey on a troop train. It wasn't a Pullman car with sleeping compartments, but the seats made up into beds at night.

It was the longest trip I had ever taken on a train. I had only ridden a little commuter train from a little town near Jackson, about six miles one way. As Boy Scouts, we would hike to the town and go to the Presbyterian Church parsonage. The pastor would mark our cards to show that we had been there. Then, we would catch the train back to Jackson for ten cents.

We traveled across North Dakota and Montana, both quite flat in the parts we went through, then Idaho, into Washington, and down to southern Oregon. In addition to us draftees, there was a large group of enlisted men who had been in the Army Specialized Training Program (ASTP). They had been attending college while studying engineering and language skills. That program had been discontinued, and these men were now being sent for basic training and further assignment.

Camp White was in southern Oregon's Rogue River Valley near Medford, Grants Pass, and Ashland. It was built on gravel soil that didn't seem fit for anything else. I later learned this was the type of land most camps were put on. To the east of Camp White, we could see Mt. Hood from our barracks windows each morning.

("Camp White was kind of a bleak place. It was like a desert out there. Only, it wasn't a lot of sand and stuff, but it was still sagebrush and stuff like that. And, the Bend Desert wasn't too far away from there, and that's where they had had some maneuvers before. So, it was a new experience for all of us guys, because we had not only the draftees but ASTP people that had come from schools." —JWZ, 2004)

We were assigned to barracks, training platoons, and squads when we arrived. Then, we were assigned bunks in the barracks according to platoon and squad. I remember I was on the second floor of the barracks, and the second story of our barracks had a balcony where we could look out at the scenery. We had arrived in February, so the early mornings and evenings were pretty cold, but the air was quite damp, making it feel even colder. On days when the sun was bright, after inspection, we would hang our bedding on the porch railings to air out.

There were eight men in a squad and four squads in a platoon. Each squad had a squad leader and assistant squad leader, and each platoon had an officer platoon leader and a platoon sergeant. I think there was a platoon assigned to each barracks for basic training. I was assigned to Company B, 2nd Platoon. Our platoon leader was 1st Lt. Robert Hanna, a West Point graduate, and our platoon sergeant was Staff Sergeant Kenneth W. Koenecke.

("We got assigned to our barracks and everything else we would need to know for the near future. I don't remember what day of the week it was when we got there. It was probably a

Thursday because I think we left Fort Snelling around Monday or Tuesday. So, it would have been a Thursday or a Friday when we got there. And, I'm sure the next week we started our basic training." —JWZ, 2004)

Basic training was conducted by NCOs from Company B of the 383rd Infantry Regiment. Some of my platoon members were Maro Learned and Darold Lidtke from Westbrook, MN; Loren Brower from Luverne, MN; Joseph Spellazza from St. Louis, MO; Eli Mandel from Huron, SD and Walter Phillips from Mitchell, SD; Louis Vogel from Cincinnati, OH; and Ray LeSeur and Paul Specht from Minneapolis, MN.

During a five-minute break on the first day of training (we would get a five-minute break each hour, generally a "smoke" break, as most of us smoked cigarettes), our platoon sergeant, Bill Koenecke, came over to a group of us and asked if any of us were from Minnesota. Several of us said we were, and he wanted to know what cities or towns we came from. When I said I was from Jackson, he wanted to know if I knew a man named Herman Koenecke. I told him Herman had been my barber, to which he replied that Herman was his father. After Bill had entered the Army, his parents had moved to Jackson from nearby Ceylon, MN, and Bill's sister and her husband lived in Jackson. His sister's husband was Lee Conlon, who worked for Joe Prevatil as a baker. I had been Joe's paperboy when I was in junior high school. It was a small world, even then.

We didn't get any passes for the first two weeks of basic training, so many of us spent our "spare" time writing letters home. During and even for a while after basic training, the lights in the barracks were turned off at ten o'clock at night, even on weekends.

I came to know Sgt. Koenecke quite well, as we talked about Jackson and Ceylon. One Sunday evening I was sitting on my bunk writing a letter when Bill came by. He had been on a pass and was returning to his room on the west end of the barracks. It was almost 10 o'clock, so he invited me to come to his room to finish writing my letter. Many nights after that I would go to Bill's room to finish a letter or just talk.

One night, when I was in Bill's room, he said he had a picture to show me. I told him I had one to show him, too. We exchanged pictures and, believe it or not, we were looking at the same picture of the same girl. We had both received a letter and picture from a girl who had moved to Jackson from Ceylon before I went into the Army. I didn't know she had moved from Ceylon, Bill's hometown. She was only a letter-writing friend to both of us, but we had a good laugh over it.

During basic training, we spent some time doing weapon familiarization. After the National Guard had been called to active duty in 1940, the Minnesota State Guard was formed, and Jackson had a unit. During my senior year in high school, I had been a member and had become familiar with the weapons the Guard used for training, learning the nomenclature and how to take them apart and reassemble them. So now, in basic training, we were doing the same thing. It didn't take long for me to learn how to do this with the M-1 rifle. One night, when we were practicing this, one of the squad leaders came by and, after watching us for a while, told me to work with the other men and teach them how to do it.

("I ended up qualifying as a sharpshooter and qualified as an expert on some weapons. It was just how good a score you got on the targets on the various ranges and so forth. Because, we'd fire for like one hundred yards, three hundred yards, five hundred yards, and they each had targets. And, it just depended on your score what you got. And then, we even had one course where we laid on our backs and fired at model airplanes. Well, that's what they were. They were targets, I guess, with airplanes on 'em, or whatever, and we used twenty-two rifles. And, I qualified as an expert on that one. And they said, 'Boy, you must have done a lot of hunting.' But I really had not." —JWZ, 2004)

We had several Native-American men (we still called them Indians, then) and Spanish-American men (we knew them as Mexicans) who were part of our basic training unit. One of these was a Native American we called "Chief." He was somewhere between the ages of 35 and 40 and said he had bad knees, which made him walk a bit stiff-legged. One day during grenade training the instructor was showing us how to safely handle and throw a hand grenade. He pulled the pin on the grenade and told us as long as we held the handle down, the grenade would not explode. When he was trying to put the pin back in, he dropped the grenade. He yelled and turned to run and so did everyone else. Then we heard him laughing, so we all stopped to see why. The grenade had not exploded because all the explosive material had been removed, and the instructor was standing there, laughing, and pointing to his right. Everyone turned to look, and there, farther away than anyone else, bad knees and all, was "Chief." I'll bet he was saying, "Knees, don't fail me now!" The instructor told us we should always hit the ground when a live grenade was dropped, ordering us, "Do not try to pick it up!!"

Another time, we were out in the field on the firing range. I had qualified as a sharpshooter with the M-1 rifle, and we also ran through some tactical problems while there. The plan was to run through the obstacle course during the day and then again after dark. It began raining in the afternoon when we were on the course, so everybody was very wet and muddy. And we were going to run it again after dark.

That evening, the temperature started to fall, and as we waited to go through the course again, someone finally built some fires to help us warm up, even if it was only one side of your body at a time. After dark, we went through the course and everyone came through okay. I mention that we all came through okay because, during this exercise, they were firing live ammo about two feet off the ground, right over where we were crawling! The only time there were any casualties was when someone would get scared and stand up, but that almost never happened, and it didn't happen for us.

Now, more tired, muddier, and even wetter, we huddled around the fires, trying to keep warm. It was now so cold our clothes were freezing stiff. We had been the last group to go through the course that day and now we were waiting (and waiting!) for the trucks to come and take us back to the main camp area. We were about five miles out from the main camp.

Finally, about midnight, the officer in charge took a jeep and went to find out where the trucks were.

When he got back, he said the trucks had all been put away for the night because they had thought they had picked up the last group. The motor pool was scrambling to get drivers to come out and pick us up. We were so wet and cold, we asked if we could start marching back to camp to try and warm up and get our circulation going. The officer agreed, so we started marching and were only about two miles from camp when the trucks arrived.

It was about three o'clock in the morning when we finally got to our barracks. I think almost everyone went into the showers, clothes and all, just to get clean and warm. But before we could go to bed, we also had to clean our rifles. The Army tells you it is your best friend and you need to take care of it or it won't take care of you.

As we were going to bed, the officer told us that we did not have to get up for reveille the next morning. When the charge of quarters came around in the morning, one of the sergeants told him to let us sleep until eight o'clock. They made special arrangements with the mess sergeant to feed us after eight o'clock.

In mid-April we completed basic training and were assigned to our permanent companies. Some of my friends were sent to different units for advanced training. Maro went to Company I, 383rd, and Darold went to Company K, 383rd; Ray LeSeur went to the 96th MPs (Military Police); Harold Bute went to another company (*I'm not sure where because I didn't see him again until after the war)*; another friend, Bob Luscombe from Oregon, went to the 361st Field Artillery. I was assigned to the 2nd squad, 2nd platoon of Company B, which would be my training company. I remember a man from Chicago named DeLuca who was assigned to the 96th MP Company. Barely five feet tall - I think he had to stand on a couple of sheets of paper to pass the height test - he couldn't understand why he was going to the MPs, but they told him when they got through training him, he would be able to handle anyone, big or small.

Sunday afternoons were usually free time. On a few Sundays, I went out to a deserted part of the camp with Jimmy Truesdale, another man in the Company, to look for agates. His hobby was collecting agates and making them into jewelry. Another man with us in Basic Training, Sam Scheiner, was a piano player from Minneapolis, who would play for us and for the dances they had there. I remember seeing his name in the Minneapolis Star Tribune after the war but I don't remember if it was for playing the piano somewhere or for something else. At least I knew he made it through the war and got back home. So many did not.

After basic training ended and before our individual training began, we could get weekend passes to Medford. One weekend, Maro and I went to go bowling duckpins. This was the first time I had ever done this. I had bowled with regular pins and even worked in a bowling alley, but these were small pins and small bowling balls without any finger holes. It was fun, but I preferred regular bowling. Other times, we would just stay in camp on the weekend and use the Company dayroom or go to the Post Exchange, where they had a recreation room.

It was hard to think about the dangerous changes that would be coming into our lives soon. For the time being, we were working and even enjoying, in some ways, this new life we had undertaken. But with the end of Basic Training, life was about to change in ways we could never imagine.

[4] Staff Sergeant Kenneth W. "Bill" Koenecke. From Ceylon, MN. Bill was wounded by Japanese gunfire on Okinawa, resulting in the loss of his left arm.

---

[4] SSgt. Kenneth W. "Bill" Koenecke. ca. 1944. Private collection.

[5]Pfc. Maro Clyde Learned in his Service Picture from 1944. Born 24 November 1925, Westbrook, MN. Died April 4, 1945, Okinawa, at 19 years of age. Buried in Cottonwood County, Minnesota.

---

[5] Pfc. Maro Clyde Learned. 1944. Private collection.

CHAPTER 2

After Basic Training

Learning New Skills

In late April, we got word that the Division Combat Teams were moving to Camp Callan in the San Diego area of southern California. Division Headquarters and the artillery units were sent to other bases in the area. We went through Sacramento on the three-day move. While I was stationed at Camp Callan, I was promoted to Private First Class, a rank I would have until after the Okinawa campaign.

After we settled into our new barracks, the Company Commander sent word for me to report to him. He told me Lt. Hanna had recommended me for voice radio school on the base. If I chose to go to the school, I wouldn't have to pull any extra duties during the four-week course. I chose the school!!

I spent most of May learning radio procedures, how to talk "radioese," voice codes, Morse code, what not to say, and other things. We went out on field problems using vehicle-mounted radios and walkie-talkies. The walkie-talkies were what the platoon radiomen, like me, would use. We were warned to watch our language because there had been instances when the messages we transmitted were received on local broadcast bands and could be heard by people listening to regular radio.

I remember going on only one weekend pass while we were stationed at Camp Callan. Maro and I went to San Diego, mainly to be doing something different. Now, keep in mind that San Diego was a Navy town. The Army MPs and the Navy Shore Patrol (SP) tried to help the local police keep order, but fights were breaking out all the time, mostly between the sailors and the Marines, but occasionally Army personnel would jump in, too. Maro and I weren't fighters, though, and so we avoided trouble. We roamed around in the stores, visited various service centers, went to the movies, and ate at some restaurants.

Late in the afternoon, we needed to make reservations at a service club so we would have a place to sleep that night. We tried them all, but they were full. So, what to do now? We went to an all-night theater. We paid for as many movies as they were showing so we could stay all night. We slept through a good portion of them.

About five o'clock the next morning, we left the theater and went looking for breakfast. Service clubs usually start serving by about six o'clock in the morning, so we found one and ate. After breakfast, we caught a bus to Balboa Park, where the San Diego Zoo is. It was a great way to spend the day, wandering through the zoo and looking at the different animals and plants. There were concession stands, so we had places to eat and buy souvenirs.

At one point, we were standing by a pen with mynah birds when we heard a shrill wolf whistle. We were startled and, looking around, saw some girls who were staring at US as they walked by. We decided we better walk away before we got into trouble not of our making. We remained in the area for a while, looking at other birds and animals. Later, we heard the wolf whistle again and realized it was the birds making the sound. I guess the girls must have thought we were whistling at them! Finally, late in the afternoon, we caught a bus that took us back to camp.

In the camp we had movie theaters, post exchanges, and company day rooms, along with athletic fields and gyms to use, so we had plenty of things to do in our off-duty hours. The units were encouraged to participate in sports, so the companies formed baseball teams and set up a schedule of games. One weekend, I was at one of the baseball games and fell asleep while lying on the ground watching. It was a hot, sunny day, and I had taken off my fatigue jacket and undershirt. When I woke up later, I had the worst sunburn I have ever had. It was a good thing I was going to radio school now because I would not have been able to wear a backpack for very long. Luckily, I was healed up by the time I had to resume normal training activities that included long marches, close-order drills, and practicing on the firing range.

When I returned to duty with the company, those of us who could not swim were sent to the pool in Del Mar, CA, for swimming lessons. On our first day, they had us line up and go out on the diving board and jump off one by one. When we surfaced, one of the lifeguard instructors would push a long pole at us and pull us to the side of the pool. After that, we held on to the side of the pool and practiced kicking our legs like we were swimming. We were supposed to have these lessons a couple of times a week, but they were stopped before we had our next lesson.

I think headquarters had received orders to step up our training, because one day we were taken to a pier that was thirty or forty feet high, and it must have been close to a hundred feet long. We were given life jackets, shown how to hold our arms and legs so we wouldn't get hurt, and told to jump off and swim to shore. This was to simulate jumping off a sinking ship. Most of us did it, but a few balked, and they were forced to jump or were pushed off. Most of us figured out that we were going on a trip on the ocean soon. (Just going to do a little sailing!)

After that, using Navy personnel landing boats near San Clemente Island, we practiced amphibious landings, both on the mainland and the island. For some reason, I never got seasick. Some people said it was because I came from Minnesota, the land of 10,000 lakes, but I don't think so! When we were out on the water, I would ride in the bow of the boat and look for jellyfish and other fish in the ocean. The water was very clear in those days; I wonder if it still is.

("We were at war, and we knew that it was serious business. And, yet, we always had fun, too, taking in new surroundings and new experiences. I think that's the American soldier: there's humor in every place you go. Sometimes in war situations is when it comes out the best." —JWZ, 2004)

When we came ashore on the last day of these landings, Bill Koenecke and I were next to a pit - dugout, square pits with logs around them - where dynamite or "Concentrated C" was exploded to simulate mortar and artillery fire. When someone was within ten feet of the pit, the person doing the exploding was not supposed to set it off. However, this time he did, and when the noise of the explosion subsided, my ears were ringing. We didn't think too much about it and went on with the exercise. It took some time, but eventually, my ears finally quit ringing. Later, I found out that my eardrums had been broken that day.

("The next day we were told to start packing our bags and stuff for going home, and to turn in all the equipment that we wouldn't be taking. Anything that we weren't taking with us home, and all our personal items. And, we had to carry our duffel bags to go home, and they can be pretty heavy. But we did." — JWZ, 2004)

All our equipment was to be turned in to the supply room. We were getting ten days of leave plus travel time which amounted to about sixteen days for me. When we came back, we would be at Camp San Luis Obispo in California.

Bill was also going on leave, so the next day, we caught the train to San Francisco, where we would make connections for the train to Kansas City, Omaha, and Worthington. When we got to San Francisco we had a layover of several hours before our train left. As young men, always thinking first of our stomachs, we went to get something to eat, then found the cable cars and took a ride.

There were some theaters near where we got off the cable car, so Bill asked if I had ever been to a burlesque theater. As I had not, we went to one. It was not at all what I had pictured. Sure, there were comedy acts and singing, and some of it was risqué, but there weren't a lot of half-naked women parading around as is depicted in magazines. We left the theater in time to catch our train and start the long journey back home to Jackson. We must have traveled by coach because we had to sleep in our seats at night.

As we crossed the mountains, my ears began to hurt and even bleed. That was the first time I realized that something bad must have happened from the beach explosion. After we got over the mountains, though, my ears felt better, and I enjoyed the rest of the trip.

Another Minnesota draftee, Paul Mazurka, from Blackduck, was on the train for part of the trip. He had been inducted with me and in basic with us but had been sent to another unit. I didn't meet up with Paul again until we were in Kansas City waiting to catch the train to Omaha. While we were waiting, I noticed Paul smiling and looking at a couple of women nearby who were talking in a foreign language. I knew Paul was of Polish descent, so I asked him if he could understand them. He laughed and said they were talking about some female problems, but they didn't realize someone could understand them!

After changing trains in Kansas City, we traveled up to Omaha and then continued north to Worthington. Our tickets were made out for some little town north of Worthington we had never heard of called Miloma, but we decided to get off at Worthington and take the bus to Jackson. *(It was a good thing we did, too, because Miloma turned out to be just a mail-stop by a grain elevator out in the country.)*

It was early in the morning when we finally got off the train, and we lucked out because when we found the bus depot it was at a restaurant, so we ate breakfast while waiting for our bus.

When we boarded the bus there were two girls from Fairmont in the seat behind us. Bill and I were both in uniform, of course, and they leaned over the back of our seat and asked all kinds of questions about Army life, and us, and even asked if we would come to Fairmont to see them. We didn't make any commitments, but they gave us their addresses anyway. I never saw either one again after I got off the bus. Bill told me later that he had called the taller girl one day while he was in Fairmont, but he said they were too young.

I went to see a doctor one day about my ears after I got home. I think I saw young Dr. Maitland, who told me the explosion on the beach had ruptured both of my eardrums. The reason they had bled on the train trip home was due to the pressure from the higher altitude as we went over the mountains. By the time we went back to California they had healed enough that they didn't bother as we went back through the mountains.

("While I was at home, we had get-togethers with the rest of the family and so forth. I visited people, went bowling, and various things like that. Before I went in the Army, I had worked at the bowling alley in town for a while. And, between graduating from high school and going into the service, I learned to bowl. And I bowled a lot! Plus, I worked part-time at the bowling alley. So, I did a lot of [bowling], and I'd meet guys that were still home. During those days, we did a lot of cruising up

and down the streets, so I suppose we did some of that, too."—JWZ, 2004)

After visiting as much family and as many friends as I could and then saying our goodbyes, my parents took me over to Worthington where I met Bill, and we boarded our train to Omaha and all points west. My dad was not one to say "I love you," but that day as we shook hands, and even hugged, I saw a glisten of tears in his eyes as we said goodbye, not knowing if we would see each other again. I knew he loved me.

("I don't know exactly what my mom thought about me going, because she hated to see anybody go to war. But I think my dad was probably proud to see that I was going. He had wanted to join the Army during World War I, but his dad wouldn't let him go because they were farming; he was needed on the farm. So, I think he was proud that I was going."—JWZ, 2004)

Upon arriving at Camp San Luis Obispo, we learned we would only be there for a few days. There were work details and classes to attend, but no physical training exercises. I went on sick call to see what could be done for my ears, but it turned out nothing could be done.

("We had tents there, with wooden sides and wooden floors and stoves. Even though this was in June, or July of '44, somehow it was cold in that place. Maybe it was because we were so close to the ocean; I don't know. But we had stoves, and we'd get up in the morning sometimes, and be almost freezing in there so we

were glad to have them. We didn't do too much while there, some forced marches and so forth." —JWZ, 2004)

A few days later we were on the move again, this time on our way to Camp Beale, out in the Mojave Desert near Marysville, CA. We had work details that went to large hangar-type buildings to build pallets and load equipment on them. All our equipment was being palletized so that it could be loaded on the ship.

When we weren't on work detail, we were indoors attending classes on various tactics, personal hygiene, and other subjects. Those of us in communications also spent time brushing up on procedures and codes.

It was so hot in the desert, some days up to 120 degrees, that we would go out on "forced" marches at three o'clock in the morning when it was cool. Forced marches were just long hikes at a very fast speed, usually with full packs on our backs. They were usually five to ten miles in length and everyone started as a platoon in formation with the taller men usually in the lead. This was very hard on the shorter men because the taller men took longer strides. As the march progressed, though, some of the taller lead men became tired and slowed down and then those that were behind would pass them. I was surprised at myself because much of the time I would end the march as one of the lead men.

("And then we'd come back in, and by ten o'clock in the morning, we'd be inside, and we would be either on detail, building the pallets or helping to get stuff to put on pallets, or

we'd be in classrooms, inside buildings where it would be cooler."
— JWZ, 2004)

One memory from Camp Beale is about one of the men, named Thompson, who, after we were told to get our hair cut short, had his head shaved. He sunburned his head so badly he had to be hospitalized. He never returned to Company B, and I don't know if he was ever sent overseas.

By July 18th the whole Division had moved into Camp Stoneman near San Francisco. Now a veil of secrecy fell over the whole Division. We could not leave camp except to go on work detail, our letters were censored, and we were not allowed to make telephone calls. Since we couldn't leave camp, it was good that we had day rooms, movie theaters, and post exchanges we could go to.

One day, Capt. Wm. Garner, the Company Commander, sent word for me to report to his office. He told me he was sorry, but he could not have me transferred out of the unit because of the injury to my ears. I was surprised because I had not asked to be transferred, and I told him so, and the matter was closed.

Before our unit left Camp Stoneman, First Sgt. Morgan was reassigned, and Capt. Garner promoted TSgt. Jack G. Corn to that position.

One day while we were in the barracks, we heard a loud rumble, the building shook, and items on the shelves by our bunks tumbled to the floor. Our first thought was, "Earthquake!" but it was an explosion on an ammunition ship a few miles away at Port Chicago near Pittsburgh, CA.

A call quickly went out for blood donors, mainly for type O and B. My blood was type A, and I was not needed. The 382nd Regiment was alerted and men were sent over to help with guard duty.

A couple of days later, on July 22nd, we were put on ferryboats and taken up the river to San Francisco. While we were on the docks, there was a band playing and soldiers milling around getting ready to board the ship. We barely had time to get a cup of coffee or milk and a doughnut before we went up the gangplank to the ship. People had come by to watch and were waving flags and banners saying, "God bless you and be with you."

("I don't even remember where or how we got to the docks - the pier - there at San Francisco. I remember being there, but whether there were trains that we had gotten onto, I can't remember. But I know that we weren't on the pier too long and the next thing you know, we were walking up the gangplanks. And, as each ship was loaded, it moved out into the bay. Then one day, after all the ships were loaded, we set sail." — JWZ, 2004)

As each ship was loaded, it sailed out into San Francisco Bay. Our convoy included five troopships plus some escort destroyers. Each troopship was armed with guns that we all hoped would never be needed. When all the ships were ready, we sailed for Hawaii.

[6] Recruiting Poster:

"ACTION! Choose Your Combat Branch"

---

[6] (US Government & Geographic Information Office Collection, 1942)

CHAPTER 3

Hawaii and Beyond

The Pacific Theater

Now, we were on our way to Hawaii. Sailing on the ocean was a new experience for many in our group, and a lot of the men got seasick, but not me. I can remember standing on the top deck watching the flying fish out on the ocean. The trip over to Hawaii from California was uneventful. We passed the time playing cards and sunning ourselves on the deck, or reading a book or magazine from the ship's library. I did have to pull kitchen police duty one day, but that wasn't an all-day job out here. I think I did it because so many of the men were seasick.

On July 24th, we arrived at Pearl Harbor. We could see Diamond Head in the distance, and when we came in to dock, the top of the battleship Arizona was visibly sticking out of the water.

("We got to Hawaii, and we came into Pearl Harbor, and I can remember, we could see Waikiki Beach and all the barbed wire that was on the shore, all along the shoreline there, as if to say, No Swimming!" —JWZ, 2004)

After we disembarked from the ship, we were loaded onto trucks and taken to Tent City by the Schofield Barracks, where we would spend several weeks.

We lived in pyramidal tents with wooden floors and sides, six men to a tent. I was in a tent with Sgt. John Summers, Bill, Smokey Jasper - the platoon runner, and a couple of other men.

("It was kind of bewildering being in all those tents, but, you learned, just like you do in any city; you learned where your area was, what street you were on, and everything." —JWZ, 2004)

One morning, Sgt. Summers complained about the heat and his groin rash. He had some lotion with "balm" in the name and wondered if it might help. Bill told him he should try it. I can still see John hollering and hopping around the tent as the lotion stung his skin. He hurried and washed it off.

We were doing tactical problems during the days. I was also put on a supply detail with another man, Pfc. Clarence Blessing. Many days, we would go into Honolulu with a truck and a driver from the motor pool to pick up supplies for the company, usually from a supply depot. This could take anywhere from an hour or two to most of the morning, and it was usually the latter. This gave us a chance to walk around the docks or go downtown to shop.

In the afternoon, we would be with the company out in the field. I recall one time we were doing tactical problems in a pineapple field close to the camp. When we had a break, we would cut pineapples off the plants, peel them with our bayonets, and eat them. It was better that we ate them than to have the tanks grind them into the ground.

Sometimes, we put canned pineapple juice in our packs so we could have it to drink on breaks. Some men put the juice in their canteens, but they soon found out it would corrode the inside of the canteen. Pineapple juice and aluminum just didn't mix.

Oahu is a mountainous island. When we drove up to Tent City, I was surprised at how many sharp curves there were and the steep drop-offs on the side of the road. These roads had literally been cut out of the sides of the mountains.

We ran many tactical problems up in those mountains. We would go out in boats and amphibious tractors to practice landings on the beaches, and then move up into the mountains.

One time, one of our BAR men (a BAR is a Browning Automatic Rifle, a light machine gun) was firing his weapon, using blanks, and nearly fell backward off a cliff. He was holding the weapon up by his shoulder, and as he fired it, it drove him backward until another man grabbed him to keep him from falling. Needless to say, he was grateful.

We could get weekend passes, and occasionally weeknight passes to go into Honolulu. There were buses we could catch out at the camp gate. I don't remember needing to pay for the bus rides, so they must have been furnished by the military.

I recall walking down the streets of downtown Honolulu and the general hustle and bustle of the city. Like any large city, it was a busy place and a hub of all kinds of activities. There were a lot of souvenir shops and places to eat, but the prices were sky-high! (At least, they seemed high to us!) I clearly remember visiting Waikiki Beach one time with all the barbed wire coils out in the water. You couldn't go swimming out there because of the wire.

One Sunday, Maro and I spent the afternoon in a park at Waikiki Beach, just relaxing and lying around. We met a sailor there who worked in the Royal Hawaiian Hotel, which the Navy had taken over. He took us to the hotel so we could see what it looked like. It was a very fancy place with Navy personnel, mostly officers, billeted on the upper floors.

("It was very ornate. Plush and so forth. The Navy had taken it over, and so they had offices and quarters for a lot of their people. Naturally, we didn't get very far into the hotel. We got into the main part, the lobby, but we didn't get into the offices, or the rooms, or anything like that. And there again, from there it was right along Waikiki Beach with the coils of wire. It was a good thing they had swimming pools there, too." —JWZ, 2004)

We also met another sailor in the park who seemed to be getting drunk. After we had talked for a while, he offered us a drink, but we quickly refused because he was drinking aftershave lotion. We got away from him as fast as we could.

We went to a movie theater at Waikiki Beach because we could see palm trees sticking out the roof. We had never seen anything like that back home! There wasn't a movie playing at the time, but they let us go in and look around. The theater was built on a concrete slab, and they had built it around the trees, leaving openings in the roof for the tree trunks. It seemed quite strange to us, but the trees that were left didn't block the view of the screen. I suppose if it rained the water fell on the floor and ran into drains.

[7] The Waikiki Theatre screen had a rainbow proscenium arching over it, and a ledge on the sides sported artificial papaya and banana trees and other tropical plants. Flanking the screen were full-size coconut palms, with concrete trunks. (Picture courtesy of Lowell Angell in the Honolulu Star-Advertiser)

(Editor's note: The Waikiki Theater was demolished in 2005. It was built in 1936 and showed its last movie in 2002. —ed.)

One weekend, I got a pass and went looking for Johnny Malone from Jackson. Someone from home had sent me his address at Fort Shafter, which was near Honolulu. I don't know how, but I found him at the post office in Fort Shafter. He was on duty but took the time to come outside, where we found some Coca-Cola and a place to sit so we could visit. (Johnny

---

[7] (Angell, Lowell, Honolulu StarAdvertiser, 2017)

went to work at the Jackson Post Office after the war. Many years later his son married my niece, Ruth Mier.)

Another time, Maro and I had been on a pass, and we got off the bus at Tent City. We showed our passes to the MP on duty at the gate, and he asked us where we were from. When I told him I was from Jackson, Minnesota, he said he was Joe Worshek's son, Dale. I told him I had gone to school with his younger brother, Rolland. After we talked for a bit, he told the other MPs he was giving us a ride to our areas. Johnny Malone and Dale Worshek were the only two men I saw from Jackson while I was gone. (Bill Koenecke was from Ceylon, near Jackson.)

Our group had now received all the jungle training we needed. The big rumor going around was that we were going to land on the island of Yap. The big question most guys were asking was, "Where the Hell is Yap?" We soon found out it was an island about a thousand miles east of the Philippines. The Island of Yap.

("Wherever that was, we were headed for it; we were going to make a landing there. So, all the combat teams went aboard troop transports first. The invasion headquarters and rear echelon people went on the LSTs because, being on the troop transport, they could get a lot more of us together for briefings about what we were going to be running into." —JWZ, 2004)

On August 21st, just under a month after arriving in Hawaii, the men began loading the ships and LSTs with all the equipment we would need for the coming battle. The LSTs

(Landing Ship, Tank) were flat-bottomed ships with bow doors that opened like French windows. These were the ships that would take us to the shore of the island, and the tank-like vehicles (Alligators) would take us ashore. There was a lot of planning involved in loading these ships because the items needed last had to be loaded first and the items needed first had to be loaded last.

After loading the ships, we climbed aboard. The assault troops went on transports where they could be gathered for briefings about the coming operation, and the service and support troops went on the LSTs. At the staging area before reaching the target, these troops would switch, thus allowing the assault troops to ride over the treacherous reef around Yap in Alligators that we would board on the LSTs. The Alligators could ride over the waves and coral reefs, enabling us to reach the beach.

On September 1st, the fully loaded fleet left Oahu and sailed to Maui for one last dress rehearsal with all units. This practice landing was necessary to ensure that all units could work together.

After we made our landing, we had to climb up a steep bank to get on the island. Once on the island, we were looking at a land covered by cacti as big as trees. The cactus had spiny needles about two to three inches long, and the needles were very sharp. We were warned to be careful of where we stepped because these needles could go right through a leather boot. After running through some practice scenarios, we dug foxholes and settled in for the night.

We found we could eat the cactus fruit, which was about four inches long and two inches around if we trimmed off about a half-inch thick layer of the outer skin. The pulp was sweet and juicy, but if you didn't cut off the outer layer, there were short spines with hooks on the end that would stick to your tongue and the inner parts of your mouth. Luckily, it didn't happen to any of us.

The next day, after sleeping in our foxholes, we went back to the beach, re-boarded the Alligators, returned to our ships, and went back to Oahu. Now we were headed for Yap for real – or, so we thought. On September 11th the LSTs sailed. Four days later the transports were on their way to Eniwetok, the jumping-off place for the assault on Yap. But Yap would never become more than a foreign name to us.

We sailed southwest of Hawaii across the Pacific Ocean. The days were warm and balmy, and we saw flying fish, porpoises, and whales. In the morning, we did calisthenics on the deck, played cards, read, wrote letters, and just sat around talking.

Several of us had received new M-1 rifles just before we left Hawaii, so we spent part of one of the first days zeroing in our rifles by shooting at targets that were towed behind the ship. I didn't think it was very productive because the waves caused the ship to rise and fall and rock sideways while you were trying to aim at the targets, but maybe that was the point. In real life, you rarely have a stationary target.

The movement of the ship was also a drawback at mealtime. On some of the ships, we used metal trays that were provided, and on others, we used our own mess gear. After getting your food, you would find a table to stand at. The tables were about eight feet long and three-and-a-half feet high. When you put your tray or mess kit on the table, you had to hold on to it, or it would slide away when the ship rocked. In stormy or rough weather, it was a serious problem.

I remember that the bunks were five high in the sleeping quarters on the transports. I always tried to get the top bunk because, in rough seas, someone was sure to get seasick, and I didn't want them above me. It wasn't usually too hard to get the top bunk because many of the men didn't want to be high up because of the motion. Each bunk had only about eighteen inches between it and the bunk above it. On the LSTs, because they had less space between decks, the bunks were only three high.

When we arrived at Eniwetok the ship lowered lifeboats to take us ashore. We were given rations for the noon meal before we headed to the island. I think it was really to give us a chance to stretch our legs and get used to walking on solid ground again. We marched up a road for a while until we came to a clearing surrounded by mostly palm trees and some tropical plants. The soil was mostly sand and didn't look as if much else would grow there. I remember seeing a deserted building, but we didn't see any people. The island had been re-taken by the Marines sometime before. After eating our noon meal and messing around for a while, we returned to our ship. For the next leg, the convoy turned more southerly, and we headed for the Admiralty Islands.

Soon after leaving Hawaii, the scuttlebutt had started flying about something big happening. We heard that some of the brass had been called to an important meeting. We would learn later that the invasion of Yap had been called off, and we were now under the command of General Douglas MacArthur and would be participating in his return to the Philippines. We were to be a part of the forces landing on Leyte Island on October 20th.

As we sailed to the Admiralty, we had classes to familiarize us with our new objective: the terrain, people, cities, and villages of Leyte and what we could expect to face from the enemy. Calisthenics and orientation sessions were held daily, along with weapon inspections. Everything needed to be in tip-top working order when we arrived.

Manus Island was our new destination, and as we sailed south, we came to the Equator. Life almost became unbearable because of the heat. I think you really COULD fry an egg on the metal deck. The hot sun made it nearly impossible to find a comfortable place to sit.

Crossing the Equator meant that King Neptune came aboard to initiate us into the Ancient Order of the Deep. I don't remember what we had to do for the initiation, but it was an enjoyable break in the routine. I still have the certificate I received.

When we reached Manus Island, we were instructed to take our duffel bags and weapons ashore with us because when we returned to the ships, we wouldn't go back to the one we had left, but instead board the LST that we would be on to complete the journey.

Manus Island was a recreation island. As such, it had tennis courts, basketball courts, ball fields, a beer garden, a movie theater, walking trails, a swimming area, and eating places for us to use. And it was all available at no charge! We spent a whole day there doing whatever we wanted. I know I spent some time in the water and on the beach. I don't recall taking in a movie, but I may have. Mostly my buddies and I just laid around relaxing and taking life easy. Nobody thought about whether this might be our last good time together. Too soon it was time to load up and head back out to the LSTs.

Our LST had all the trucks, jeeps, and alligators that we would need once we hit the beach at Leyte. Even though we were loaded and ready, we still had a long way to go before we would get off this ship. We were assigned to bunks in the sleeping quarters. Since it was very hot, some of the men opted to sleep down below on the tank deck. I couldn't understand why because, with this flat-bottomed ship, you could feel every wave it hit, especially if you were below. Some of the men who stayed down there were sick for much of the voyage. Most of us spent long days on the main deck, and some of the time we even stayed there at night, too. It was much cooler up on deck than it was below.

I remember when we boarded the LST we had to climb up cargo nets to get on deck. This is quite a job, and even more so if you have not done it before. You must be ready to catch the cargo net with your hands when the lifeboat rises on the waves. Timing is everything. If you grab the net when the boat is down you are in danger of getting your legs smashed between the boat and the ship when the waves push the boat up. Most of us were able to do this all right, though, and no one was hurt.

However, when we were climbing up the net to board the LST, I was right over the diesel exhaust. This would have been OK if we had been able to keep moving up, but for some reason, the men on the net above me stopped, and I was stuck right over the exhaust with no place to go. When I finally got up on deck, I was quite sick for a while from the diesel fumes. That was the only time I was sick while on a ship.

Once again, our days were taken up with calisthenics, classes, and maintaining our weapons, usually in the mornings, while our afternoons were free, mostly spent playing cards (hearts, whist, euchre, cribbage, pinochle, and poker), writing letters, or just talking. In addition to our Army troops, sailors fully manned the ship. Sometimes, when the order came for the sailors to mop down the deck, we would grab mops and help them. We also helped the sailors get their guns ready when the order came for them to "man their guns." Most of the guns we helped with were 20 and 40 millimeters. I think we all knew we were fighting the same war against common enemies, so there was a kind of camaraderie among all the men on board. Quite different from some of the bars and clubs when sailors and soldiers mixed together!

The ship's loudspeakers were on during the day with music and news except during "general quarters," the alert for the crew of some type of danger, such as submarines, which were a daily concern. Another everyday occurrence was "Tokyo Rose," the name given to English-speaking Japanese radio broadcasters whose programs were aired in the South Pacific to demoralize the troops. She told us one day that the LST sailing right behind us had been sunk, and later that day, she said our ship had also been sunk. God must have helped us because we were still on top of the water.

We were now sailing northwest, headed toward the Philippines. We left Manus Island on October 11th, and the landing on Leyte was set for October 20th, just nine days away.

CHAPTER 4

Leyte

The Reason That We Trained

October 20th was a bright, clear day as we entered Leyte Gulf. Two days before we arrived, a Ranger Battalion had made landings on two small islands at the entrance to the gulf. They had cleared the islands, and at the same time, the Naval bombardment of Leyte had begun. Our combat team was to land on Blue Beach near the town of Dulag. Heavy bombardment of this area had begun at 9:15 a.m. from the guns on the big battleship Tennessee, three cruisers, and a destroyer. Also, a thirty-nine-minute barrage of rocket and chemical mortar shells from small LCIs (Landing Craft Infantry) swept the island.

At ten o'clock, the LSTs moved onto the beaches, their bow doors opened, and, already loaded, the alligators came out, and we were on our way. It was very quiet in the alligator as we moved toward the beach. I think it was probably one of the worst days of the war for most of us; not knowing what we were going to find or what was going to happen. I know I was scared and I think the others were too.

("I believe anyone who says he is not scared when going into battle is a liar or a fool. —JWZ, 2004")

I was riding in the bow of the craft, right against the ramp that would be lowered, and Lt. Hanna was next to me. We would be the first two men to leave the alligator. You could see some of the men praying and others who were grimly silent. We were all crouched down just waiting for the first bullets to hit our craft or fly overhead. We went across the beach and into the jungle. We could see the palm trees overhead. Finally, Lt. Hanna told the driver to stop. He knew we were further in than we were supposed to go. Just before the ramp was lowered, I felt the sting of a bullet hitting the ramp. It may have been a ricochet from one of our troops or it could have been fired from the enemy.

When the ramp went down, we went out of the alligator, each one going to the right or left when we got on land. We fanned out and took cover, waiting for Lt. Hanna to give us our orders. To our great surprise, there were no Japanese troops or resistance to our landing. We cautiously began to move forward through the jungle. In three-quarters of an hour, we had moved inland over a thousand yards with no sight of any enemy. There had been some sporadic mortar and artillery fire, but we had not lost any men.

("I remember that we went in a lot further than we were supposed to. Finally, Lieutenant Hanna, our platoon leader, had to tell the guys to stop, because we were far ahead of everyone else. What shooting we did hear that first day could have been from some of our own people because they were behind us."—JWZ, 2004)

As we pushed forward into the jungle, we found swamps that were sometimes hip-deep. Sometimes, men would sink in the swamp, but there was always a buddy close by to help them out and get them on the move again. Packs and gas masks were discarded and put in a pile for later pickup. Only the essentials were kept.

For food, we had an assault ration - a large chocolate bar about 4 inches long and 1 inch square and hard as a rock - and K-ration packages. These were easy to carry along with our rifle, ammunition, and a poncho. Ponchos were better than raincoats because they could be opened up and spread out for ground cover or used as a shelter. In our backpacks, we had spare socks and other personal items, and attached to the pack was the new Army shovel that would also serve as a pick when digging in hard ground.

We were at the base of Catmon Hill, where the Japanese artillery and mortars that were giving us trouble had been placed. It was decided that our regiment would take Catmon Hill and secure it. The 1st Battalion, of which we were a part, would go up the face of the hill, the 2nd and 3rd Battalions would each take a flank, and together, we would use a pincer movement to attempt to take the hill.

Before we could move into position at the base of the hill, though, we had to cross the Liberanan River. Some of the amphibious tractors were with us to help us cross the river. Capt. Garner, our company commander, and some other men went across to scout the terrain and determine where to position the company. Soon, we heard machine-gun fire, quickly followed by a call for medics. It seems one of the gunners on another tractor had seen movement in the jungle across the river and had opened fire. It turned out to be Capt. Garner and the other men. Several of them were wounded, including Capt. Garner. They were taken to a hospital ship. We never saw Captain Garner again.

It was already getting dark, so our platoon was sent out on a scouting patrol of the terrain off to our right. We were part of a composite group with elements from C Company and were led by Capt. Hugh Young, of C Company. We had to move through the thick underbrush, and as we went, we knocked out two machine guns and reached the top of the ridge.

After we had secured the ridge, we were ordered off again to make way for a naval bombardment of the whole area. We worked our way down the hill to the river and dug in on the slope.

That night, there was a Japanese air raid on the ships offshore. Some of us climbed partway up the hill and sat, watching the battle. We could see the tracer bullets flying through the air and the anti-aircraft fire from the ships. The planes that were hit would explode, sometimes in the air and sometimes when they hit the water. We could see some of the ships get hit, too. It was almost like watching the 4th of July fireworks, except this one was having terrible consequences. After the Japanese airplanes had been driven off, the Naval bombardment began and continued for a long time.

The following morning, October 21st, we crossed the river, returned to the battalion, and pushed off. A and C companies were the attack companies, with Company B in reserve. With continual artillery fire and direct fire from the battalion anti-tank platoon, we were able to work our way through a maze of pillboxes and trenches. By late afternoon, the battalion was able to consolidate its position. We were immediately faced with a Japanese counterattack, but by calling on the three artillery battalions, we drove off the attack.

For the next three days, the battalion maintained its position on the hill and conducted extensive patrolling. During this period, we were supplied with rations and ammunition by hand; the carrying parties consisted mostly of cooks. Sadly, we lost a couple of men to "friendly fire" during those three days.

We were dug in on the hill, and everybody was supposed to stay in his foxhole after dark. Anything that moved was shot, whether man or beast; several wild pigs and carabao (water buffalo) were killed. We all knew that no one was to get out of his foxhole after dark for any reason. I don't know if they ever did find out why Lt. Dick Williams and Sgt. Jack Corn got out of their foxhole, but during the night, we heard some shots. In the morning, we discovered their bodies just a few feet from their foxhole. Everyone was shaken up because they were both really good officers.

While we were dug in on Catmon Hill, I shared a foxhole with Bill Koenecke, Lt. Hanna, and TSgt. Ernest Gerstner, who was sort of a platoon CP.

("It seems like Sergeant Summers was around there with us here, too. As a radioman, I was around more with non-commissioned officers and commissioned officers than I was with

the other guys. Smokey Jasper, the runner, and I shared a hole sometimes." —JWZ, 2004)

We actually had two foxholes, not one, but they were close together. We also had a hand-cranked telephone in the foxhole so we could communicate with the rest of the company. In the foxholes, one man would stand guard while the other one slept, changing off every two hours during the night so we all could get some rest.

One night, while I was on guard, the telephone started to move up the side of the foxhole. I took hold of it and pulled it back down. Soon it started to move again, so this time, I just stopped it, and while I held it, I called the company CP. They said someone else was having the same problem and passed the word for everyone to be on the alert. Nothing else happened that night, so we figured it must have been an animal that had been feeding and had become tangled in the telephone wire. Who knows?

On October 27th, our Company, along with the mortars and machine guns of Company D, advanced on Labir Hill under the command of Colonel List, Battalion Commander. Before we reached the crest of the hill, the Japanese unleashed a hail of machine-gun and mortar fire so intense we were forced to withdraw. The D Company Commander and the Battalion S-3 were killed along with seven other men. Col. List and 32 others were wounded. Major King took over command of the battalion. I think all the other men killed were from B Company.

The last man to withdraw from the hill was Sgt. Alonzo Self, a mortar-man from B Company. As he withdrew, he was delivering covering fire from his BAR as five Japanese soldiers followed him. Although wounded, he kept firing and killed all five of the enemy before he was killed. For this act of courage, he received the Silver Star Medal posthumously.

The 381st Regiment was then called up from reserve, pushed through our positions, moved into position at the base of the hill, and dug in for the night. We had heavy rain that night. I had been sleeping and suddenly awoke cold and wet. My foxhole was filling up with water from the rain. We couldn't get out of our holes, so we had to bundle up as best as we could to wait for the morning. Even in the tropical Philippines, it can get cold at night, especially if you're wet. Strangely, we didn't get sick from all the times we got wet and cold. Anyway, it seems most of their men were not carrying ponchos or raincoats, and one man, who had carried his poncho, was offered as much as seventy-five dollars for it, but he refused.

The next day, October 28th, after a heavy bombardment of the Japanese positions, the 381st made their way to the top. There was very little resistance from the enemy that day. Apparently, after the attack by the 1st Battalion, 383rd, the Japanese had sustained enough casualties to realize their situation was hopeless, as they withdrew their forces from Catmon Hill and moved back toward Dagami.

After Catmon Hill was secured, Bill led a party of men back to the site of our attack to recover the bodies of those we had lost. He told me later it was one of the hardest things he had done. He said it was because when the Division was in training in Oregon, a man named Lloyd Staggs was killed when he stood up in his foxhole as a tank drove over it. Bill had escorted the body back to his family in Tennessee. One of the men killed during our attack on the hill had been Lloyd's twin brother, Floyd Staggs. Bill participated in the burial of both men.

("Sergeant Staggs probably made it so the rest of us could get back out of there because he cleaned out some machine guns. But he got killed doing it. I mean he was - he had a BAR, Browning Automatic Rifle - and he was firing to keep them down while we tried to move back. He was acting as our rear-guard force, but he got shot and killed, too." —JWZ, 2004)

Following the capture of Catmon Hill, we pulled back down to the beach area, where we were loaded on trucks. We then moved through the secured town of Tabontabon and into the Dagami area, where we set up our positions near Tingib by the Binahaan River.

The 96th Division's job was to mop up any pockets of resistance by the Japanese that had been bypassed earlier and to completely rid our area of the enemy.

("We checked out the little villages, and there wasn't much damage to those. The natives were always glad to see us. They'd come out to greet us, even when we were on patrol. We'd come into a clearing, and there'd maybe be four, five, six houses, or maybe more. And, they'd come out to greet us, and we'd ask if they had seen any Japanese. Generally, it was no. Sometimes, the guys would buy chickens from them or something. But, on the other hand, they'd come to us, bring us bananas and coconuts and things like that. Or they'd go up in our trees, where we were,

and get them for us, the coconuts, that is, way up high in the trees." —JWZ, 2004)

We didn't know it, but 60,000 Japanese reinforcements had landed on the other side of the island, at Ormoc. Meanwhile, our 3rd and 7th Fleets had nearly annihilated the Japanese fleet. Now, in addition to cleaning up pockets of resistance, we also had to block the mountain passes coming from the Ormoc Valley to keep the Japanese in the valley where the 7th Division and the 24th Division could encircle them in a pincer movement.

("In Ormoc, we had outposts up on these high hills, and the only way they could get supplies was that someone had to bring it up to them. And it usually took a company to do this. I can remember going on those trails, starting out in the early morning and traveling up and down these hills, carrying cases of ammo, or cases of food and stuff on your back. It'd take all day to go up there and back." —JWZ, 2004)

From our positions near Tingib, we sent out daily patrols to scout the area ahead. Our greatest danger was snipers up in trees and enemy patrols out looking for us. It was about this time the Filipinos offered to scout for us. The Filipinos hated the Japanese with a passion, and most of these men had fought a kind of guerrilla war against them after the islands were occupied. These men carried wicked-looking "Bolo" knives in addition to Japanese rifles they had "confiscated." Those "Bolo" knives were razor-sharp, too! While we were on patrol, these scouts would suddenly disappear. When this happened, the patrol would immediately take cover and wait. Before too long, the scouts would reappear, carrying the head of a Japanese soldier between them. I think they took the heads to their village and were rewarded well.

We encountered several banzai attacks while we were in this area. We had placed machine guns around the perimeter, with crossing zones of fire, along with mortars, BARs, and riflemen in the foxholes. We could hear the Japanese before they attacked; it sounded like they were psyching themselves up. They would come across the river in the dark, screaming, yelling, and horns blowing, but we would put up flares, and when they came, they would be caught in the crossfire of the machine guns and rifles. We didn't lose any men doing this, and a lot of the Japanese died.

When we went out on patrol, we sometimes came to a clearing, and we would find about a dozen thatch houses there. These houses were built on poles, with the floor about three feet off the ground. Under the houses, you could see chickens or pigs, and sometimes a dog or two would also be there.

("We went out on patrols, and checked areas, and a couple of times we came back with some chickens that we found and had 'liberated' from the woods." —JWZ, 2004)

The houses would usually be in two rows, with a courtyard in the middle. In front of the houses would be woven mats, probably made from palm branches, and on these mats would be rice or other crops that were drying. The natives would come out to greet us, dressed in light-colored clothes, men usually wearing shorts and women long, light-colored dresses. They were very happy to see us! We would ask if they had seen any

Japanese in the area or any other American patrols. Usually, the answer was negative. I never could understand how the Filipinos could sit with their buttocks resting on the back of their legs, and sit like that for hours.

We stayed in this area long enough so that the natives came around, and the women would ask if they could, "You're your clobes, Joe?" or bring us bananas or coconuts. We all had clothes to wash. It only cost a few pesos, and at least we would have clean fatigues and socks. The natives also built us shelters made from woven palm branches over our tents. This helped to camouflage our tents and keep the Japanese pilots flying overhead from seeing our positions.

One day when we heard planes overhead, and we stopped to look, we saw one of our P-38s fighting a Japanese Zero. They were making all sorts of aerial maneuvers and were shooting at each other. Our P-38s were something to watch! We heard noises on the ground around us, and, looking closer, we saw links from machine gun ammo belts that were hitting the ground around us. They were from the planes above and were going into the ground several inches when they hit, making us realize we needed to have our helmets on and be under some heavy cover.

We had a large tent set up with camouflage netting over it. This tent was used for the kitchen. Our cooks had been brought up from the rear, and we were having some hot meals now. One day we heard some yelling in the kitchen and saw the cooks and KPs come running out of the tent. When we went to see what was going on, we found that a snake, about six feet long and three inches in diameter, had slithered into the tent. It came in one side, and, when the cooks saw it, everybody went out the opposite side. Someone went in and shot the snake, and everything was fine again. The natives nearby came and told us the snake was not poisonous, and they took it away, for food, probably.

We were able to bathe in the river because it was quite shallow. Not baths, because we didn't want to be caught without our clothes on, but we could wash our face and hands, sometimes our feet, and shave. A lot of us were only eighteen and nineteen, so we didn't shave very often. Along with having our clothes washed, this made us more livable with each other.

I don't remember who I shared a tent with during this time, but all the men got along well, mainly because we had learned we had to depend on each other. We were kept busy with our patrols, our rations were brought to us by truck or jeep after the engineers built a road, and we received mail from home. I also remember meeting with some of the other men to read our Bibles and have a type of worship service because the chaplain didn't get to us very often.

It was during this period that I woke up one day and did not feel well. I finally went on sick call and was sent to a hospital. I had yellow jaundice (hepatitis A) and hookworms, which came from walking in the wet, filthy swamps. The medics gave me three gelatin capsules about an inch long and a half-inch in diameter, filled with some type of gas that was supposed to burn the hookworms out of the lining of the stomach. The hospital had a latrine with seats just like in the outhouses we used to have at home. Only the section I was to use was a three-holer because I wasn't the only patient with these symptoms.

(When the gas did its work, you needed to use the latrine NOW!)

I don't remember if I received any other medication, but I was there for three days and then returned to my company. Because of my hepatitis, I can't give blood, even today. Once, when I asked why, the doctor told me that I needed it myself.

The biggest fight we had at this time was when T/Sgt. Donald Scott led the 3rd Platoon to Sarisari during an intense rainstorm. They found 31 Japanese soldiers eating in a shack and killed them all by a charge with six BARs shooting at top speed. None of our men were wounded or killed.

The terrain around us was rugged. The trails ran up and down in an endless series of ridges and gorges. The jungle was thick, providing ideal spots for Japanese ambushes. The altitude was high, the clouds hung in a low mist, and it was usually raining. Altogether, it was about the least pleasant place one could imagine.

After a few days of steady rain, the roads began to disintegrate. The 321st Engineers began to construct a new road from Jaro, to be called "May Drive" in honor of our Regimental Commander, Col. Edwin T. May. They kept pushing this road closer and closer to the front lines until they were almost there by Christmas. The front line was at White Chalk Ridge.

Outposts were established upon these ridges and peaks, and I recall one time our platoon left early one morning, still dark, to carry ammunition and boxes of rations up and down steep ridges and gullies to the men on duty at an outpost. We climbed up these ridges, moving through the clouds, and continually on the alert for Japanese patrols or snipers. We took short breaks every hour so the men could rest a little, and have a cigarette. When we finally arrived at the outpost, we delivered the boxes we had been carrying, collected the information they had for us, and were soon on our way back. It was a long, tiring journey, and we were glad when we were back in our area. It was an all-day trip, and each trip usually involved a whole company. The men began to tire out from the long, hard marches, and some got jungle rot from the dampness and filth along the trail. I still have a scar on my left leg where I had jungle rot right at the top of my boot.

We were in this area when Thanksgiving came, and imagine our surprise when our company cooks made us a Thanksgiving Dinner with turkey, dressing, and all the trimmings. Made us all think of home and our families.

While we were here, we even had an opportunity to go to a water point, a place by a river where the engineers set up pumping equipment and pumped water into large tanks where it was filtered and chlorinated. This was where our drinking water also came from. They also set up enclosed shower units and some type of water heaters. We had hot showers and a shave. Even though the days were hot, it felt really good to take a hot shower! And truthfully, a lot of us didn't have the chance to shave too often.

We continued to stay in this area doing routine patrols and carrying rations and ammunition to the outpost on Mount Laao. I recall we had a Christmas ham dinner at our position at Tingib, and several men got sick from stomach poisoning. Needless to say, there was a lot of movement to the latrine we had built. We had set up our two-man tents with Company A on one side and our tents on the other. A wide "street" ran between them. I was in the last tent, and the latrine was past my tent. I could hear the people moving past my tent during the night and thought I was not going to be sick, but I was wrong.

After our battalion was relieved from active fighting, we put up a volleyball court in part of the company area. We were encouraged to take part in sports and other activities. I guess I must have participated too vigorously because I had my nose broken while playing volleyball one day. One of my friends, Joe Spellazza, was playing the row in front of me, and when he came back for a ball, I was coming forward, and his elbow connected with my nose. 'Nuff said!

I went to the aid station, to a medical clearing station, and finally to a hospital unit near the beach. I was sent to a ward, and two days later, I saw a doctor and had my nose set. He had me sit in a chair like a barber chair, and putting his thumbs on each side of my nose, he pushed until it looked straight. He told me it had already started to knit together. It did hurt, but I think he did a pretty good job.

I was there for a few days, but while I was there the brother of a girl I had met, when I was home on leave, came to see me. His sister had asked him to look me up. Also, while I was there, Bill was in the hospital for something, so we would get together at times.

While I was at the hospital, a doctor checked my ears and saw the scars from the rupturing of the eardrums. He kept me at the hospital a bit longer, so he could try to make them work by using some type of suction method to force the eardrums to move. It never seemed to help and finally, I returned to my company.

I recall we were there when the battle for Luzon was started. When the prison camps on Luzon were opened by our troops, they began sending the prisoners-of-war (POWs) to Leyte for medical examinations and care before they sent them home. Bill and I spent some evenings on the beach relaxing by the bonfires that were built, and talking with some of them, most of them were women and children. They told us about the conditions in the prison camps and how the Japanese treated the prisoners. We commented that many of the men we had seen had a foot or leg missing, and they told us the Japanese had amputated them so the men would not try to escape. They also told us stories of women being raped, and children being killed just because they cried or made a noise that irritated the Japanese. These former POWs did not stay at the hospital very long. They all were anxious to go home to the States and were so happy to be released.

In January, while we were still doing the mopping-up phase in the Alto Peak area, the 381st and 382nd Regiments had units that were sent to the neighboring island of Samar. Samar had only been lightly defended by the Japanese and had been retaken by the 1st Cavalry Division. The elements of the 382nd were there to support the Naval installations there, and the 381st relieved the elements of the 1st Cavalry that were still there. These troops remained there in January.

One of the men in my company wrote the following poem. We all thought it was very appropriate. A lot of us did not appreciate the way Gen. Douglas MacArthur treated us. Oh, yes, he was a brilliant soldier and tactician, but he was a pompous individual, too.

LEYTE LAMENT

(By a G.I. Joe of the 96th)

Since the twentieth day of October

Like a cold and deadly cobra

We've chased the Japs from Leyte Gulf to Ormoc.

Through the stinking swampy potholes

And the filthy native thatches

We've been making like

Der Blitzkrieg under Wehrmacht.

Now, it isn't that we're beefing

About the chow, nor sitting grieving

For all the stuff that's missing in the mails.

And it isn't that we're crying

About the G.I. clothes we're buying

From the natives — just to cover up our tails.

No, the troubles come from early

On a morning dewy — pearly,

When a mighty General faced the Leyte head.

"I'll be back," our hero shouted

"I'll be back," his echo flouted,

And the whole world trembled at those words.

No, the fly that's in the ointment

Is that in making this appointment

The mighty one forgot old G.I. Joe.

Sure, we know that Joe's a crumb

He's thick and kinda dumb —

But he's always there when

Someone says, "Let's go!"

And so it was at Leyte,

With our bright and shiny Navy,

That they shoved old G.I. Joe upon the shore.

And they shouted and applauded

From the distance, even lauded,

As he fought his way through blood

And guts and gore.

Now that Uncle Sam's the winner

And the great one is eating dinner,

He can proudly stand and raise a potent toast

To the fulfillment of his promise,

To the victor's mantle on us,

But didn't G.I. Joe make good the boast?

And so we say in parting

Since the next round is nearly starting

And not to interrupt the General's glee,

But, wouldn't it have been truer -

A little more red, white, and bluer -

To have interposed for "I" a great big "WE!"

When General MacArthur came ashore, two days after we landed, he was taken by motorcade to Tacloban, the capital city of Leyte. He could have come onto shore without getting his feet wet, but since it was a photo opportunity, they brought him partway in, and then he waded the rest of the way so the photographers could take their pictures. The 96th Division Headquarters was situated at Tacloban. When Gen. James Bradley, the Division Commander, briefed MacArthur, he showed him a map giving our positions. MacArthur told Bradley that he must have been mistaken about where he thought we were because it was all swamp where Bradley was pointing to on the map.

Bradley said, "That's where we were supposed to go, and that's where we are!"

Even while we were still engaged in flushing out the enemy, the Division command post and Gen. Bradley's staff began drawing up plans for an operation known as "Iceberg." It was a peculiar term for an ordeal by fire.

Iceberg was OKINAWA.

[8] "We of the 96th Division have a clearly defined task. It is to become a well-trained combat division in the shortest time possible. We must keep our eyes, our thoughts, on that goal. Any time spent on efforts which do not lead to that goal is time wasted and we have no time to waste. This is the kind of division we are going to be: well-trained, tough - physically and mentally, ready and eager to fight, not for personal glory or

---

[8] (Hill, William R. *In Honor of Maj. Gen. James L. Bradley*, 1944)

advancement, but for the honor of the division and the service of our country. We kill or we get killed."

—Major General James Lester Bradley

CHAPTER 5

Operation Iceberg

Our Assignment

Few of us had ever heard of this obscure island called Okinawa. A careful look at the maps made it very clear that it held the key to victory over Japan. The Japanese had heavily fortified the island, and it was close to China, Formosa, and many smaller islands where the Japanese still had troops. Enemy airpower could strike us with overwhelming strength, and what was left of the Imperial Fleet was somewhere to the north.

Okinawa was shaped like a snake, 67 miles long and 3 to 10 miles wide. The northern portion, above the narrow Chimu peninsula, was rough, mountainous, and unimportant to us. It was the southern portion that interested us: a half-a-dozen airfields in varying stages of construction lying among low hills. Most of the island's 430,000 residents lived in the vicinity of Naha, the capital and chief port. The city itself had 65,000 people. The fortress city of Shuri, which housed the Japanese Army headquarters, was in the middle of the island, and the port city of Yonaburu was on the opposite side of the island. The three formed a 5-mile arc across the island. The island was surrounded by coral reefs and doubly defended around most of its perimeter by an ancient seawall. There were no beaches on the Pacific Ocean side or the southern end of the island, so the decision was made to land our forces on the China Sea beach.

Four divisions would be in the assault: 7th and 96th Army, 1st Marine, and 6th Marine. The Army 77th would make landings on the smaller islands, and then be in reserve. The 2nd Marine Division would also be in reserve after feinting a landing on the southern Pacific side. The Army 27th Division and 81st Division would be "on call," ready to move to Okinawa if needed. We were all part of the new Tenth Army under the command of Lt. Gen. Simon B. Buckner, Jr., and part of the 24th Corps.

Our platoon leader, Lt. Hanna, had left us to go to the hospital to visit his father, who was a Colonel in the medical corps, and to have some dental work done. We never saw him again. ("I did receive a letter from him after the war, though. He was living in Arizona. – JWZ, 2004)

Our new platoon leader was Lt. John Restuccia. T/Sgt. Ernest Gerstner was promoted to First Sergeant of our Company, and Bill became the new platoon sergeant. I became Lt. Restuccia's radioman.

The Division received its orders on February 8, 1945, and two days later we were relieved of all tactical responsibility in the Philippines. Never did any outfit have a shorter time to prepare for a major operation. Six weeks remained before we would board the ship and training had to be jammed into that period, plus the long and complicated business of loading the ships and whatever rest might be possible. On top of that, we were under-strength. We did receive some replacements, but we were not at full strength when we landed on Okinawa.

Training of the new men consisted mostly of patrols against the Japanese on Leyte, even though we were not responsible for combat operations. These men needed the training and opportunity to meld into the company. Particular attention was paid to tank and infantry coordination, flamethrower, and demolition work, all of which later proved to be of vital importance. We also had a problem getting supplies for the operation because the battle for the Philippines was still going on at Luzon and other islands. We went into combat short of some supplies, but thanks to the 10th Army re-supply efforts, we were not seriously affected.

General Bradley selected the 381st and 383rd Regiments to make the assault. The 383rd was given the uncomfortable task of landing on the southern flank of the entire Tenth Army with orders to move south and seek out the enemy's main line of defense.

Two landing exercises were held to perfect Army-Navy coordination in loading, assembling, and dispatching assault craft. On March 25th, LSTs carrying the assault infantry of the 7th and 96th weighed anchor from Leyte Gulf, and two days later, the balance of the task force sailed for the target.

The trip was uneventful with low, cloudy skies shielding the convoy during the entire voyage. Aboard the ships, there was a quiet, barely noticeable tenseness that always marks an invasion-bound fleet. The men pored over maps and literature on Okinawa, played various card games, cleaned their weapons with extreme care, went to church, and wrote their last letters home. On every ship, Army and Navy personnel teamed up to put out newspapers - ours was the Deadeye Dispatch - most of them bursting with the humor that is the American fighting man's greatest asset in moments of peril.

By day, there was little drama as we moved toward the second meeting with our destiny, but at night, on the blacked-out decks, the awful majesty of war could be felt with the impact of a sledgehammer. As the darkened convoy sailed silently through the night, it was as though an unseen hand had pulled a switch, and we knew there was no turning back.

As dawn broke over the China Sea that Easter Sunday, April 1, 1945, the whole fleet lay in position offshore. Overnight, the clouds had vanished, giving way to a clear, bright morning. Recon planes hovered over the island, while other planes flashed down out of the blue to deliver loads of bombs on the beaches. We could hear the booms and see the flashes of the big guns as the battleships and cruisers rained their deadly fire on the targets onshore. Hundreds of boats and landing craft jockeyed for position, and then the strange and terrible Easter parade got underway.

In the hours just before the assault, the bombardment swelled, and one minute before 8 a.m., the first waves of assault craft were on the way. While we were on our way, racing shoreward, the rocket and mortar craft that were close in unleashed their shells on the beach. I had never seen such a sight before; the sky was filled with rockets and mortar shells streaking overhead.

H-hour had been chosen at high tide so the assault craft could get over the reef. We got over the reef, but then our craft came upon rocks that were too big for them to go over. Moving our tank up to one of these rock ledges, we put up short ladders and climbed up on the land. I think this was a part of the ancient seawall. As we clambered up onto land, only a half-hour had passed since the assault began.

Naval gunfire had blasted holes in the seawall, and now both land and amphibious tanks and DUKW-mounted chemical mortars came following immediately behind us. Demolition teams landed with the first waves and lost no time in blasting more holes in the wall.

We had steeled ourselves to meet almost anything except the Sunday calm that greeted us. Scarcely a shot was fired as we fanned out from the beach. We encountered two machine guns as we moved inland, and quickly dispatched them with grenades and BARs. By nightfall, we had moved almost two miles inland, and, as we were to learn later, as far south as we were supposed to get after three days. I was surprised to see hills covered with various colored flowers as we moved inland. They made me think of Easter back home. This was only the first day, though, and there was no way to know what lay ahead of us.

As darkness fell, word came down from the scouts in the lead that we would have to move through a minefield before we could dig in for the night. We had to be careful to stay on the path that had been cleared through the field. We crossed it successfully, each man placing his left hand on the shoulder of the man in front of him, and then moved up on a hill where we dug in for the night.

The medical services had told us that Okinawa would be an unhealthy place. We were told not to drink the water unless we purified it, to take our atabrine tablets daily, and to be on the lookout for snakes, which were supposed to be plentiful and poisonous. Instead, we found the island to present no health problems, and the snakes never materialized.

The next morning, as we got ready to move forward, we could see the rolling terraced hills and neat checkerboard farmlands. This was a place of serene beauty, and the brisk spring weather was a change from the hot, humid days in the Philippines.

The hill we had dug in on gave us a fairly clear view of the beach. In stark contrast to the serenity of the farmland surrounding us, we saw Japanese kamikaze planes trying to fly into the ships in the harbor. Some of them succeeded, while several crashed into the sea. One plane landed on the beach intact, and the pilot was captured.

There was some opposition the second day, but it was scattered, and we continued to move south. Late in the day, Lt. Restuccia led an attack against about thirty Japanese entrenched in tombs and pillboxes. I was his radioman and continued to move forward with him. The lieutenant was wounded three times in that battle.

As we fired at the enemy, Sgt. Carlos Sanchez, on my right, yelled that he had been hit. We had been receiving a lot of enemy rifle and machine-gun fire, as well as some mortar rounds. I looked over at Sanchez and saw blood covering the left side of his face. I thought he had been shot in the eye. Lt.

Restuccia, who was on my left, told me to lie still and call for a medic. Trying to crawl over me to get to Sanchez, Lt. Restuccia was hit again. The medic came, and we moved both men back to where the medic could have some protection while he attended to their wounds.

He bandaged Sanchez's head, covering his eyes, and did what he could for Lt. Restuccia. We called for a litter to get Lt. Restuccia back. Sanchez could walk but needed someone to lead him, so when the litter came, we got them back to a medical evacuation point.

While we were waiting for the litter, the medic pointed at my left leg. My fatigues were torn, and some blood was running down my leg. He checked my leg, told me I had a piece of shrapnel in it, and put a tag on my jacket to indicate I had been wounded. I had not even felt the wound, maybe because of what was happening to the others. The medic gave both Sanchez and me something to drink while we waited for the litter.

We loaded Lt. Restuccia onto the back of a medical jeep and helped Sanchez into it. Then the medics told me to get into the jeep, too. I had thought they would just clean out my wound, bandage it, and send me back. Whatever the medic had given Sanchez and me to drink must have been a sedative because I don't remember the drive to the beach, being taken out to the hospital ship, or anything until the next morning.

When I awoke, the first person I saw was a lady dressed in white. For a moment, I was befuddled, but then I remembered the day before. When the nurse saw that I was awake, she came over and asked if I wanted something to eat. I was hungry, but first, I asked her about Lt. Restuccia and Sanchez. When she came back with the food, she told me Lt. Restuccia had died during the night, and that Sanchez's wound was not serious.

I felt sad about Lt. Restuccia, in part because I thought I had contributed to his death. I thought maybe my having the radio had alerted the Japanese that he was an officer, so they had zeroed in on our position. This bothered me for a time, but later I realized that my radio antenna could not be seen very well from a distance because it was all painted olive drab and had no shiny parts. Later, I learned that Lt. Restuccia had been awarded the Distinguished Service Cross (DSC) for his gallant leadership in action. His was the first of nine DSCs earned on Okinawa.

"The President of the United States takes pride in presenting the Distinguished Service Cross (Posthumously) to John Restuccia (0-1296903), First Lieutenant (Infantry), U.S. Army, for extraordinary heroism in connection with military operations against an armed enemy while serving with Company B, 383rd Infantry Regiment, 96th Infantry Division, in action against enemy forces on 2 April 1945, in the Ryukyu Islands. First Lieutenant Restuccia's intrepid actions, personal bravery, and zealous devotion to duty at the cost of his life exemplify the highest traditions of the military forces of the United States and reflect great credit upon himself, the 96th Infantry Division, and the United States Army.

—Headquarters, Tenth U.S. Army, General Orders No. 142"

I hadn't expected to see Sanchez again, but he came back to the company. He said a bullet had hit his helmet, and a piece of the helmet had hit him just above his left eye, causing all the bleeding.

I only stayed on board the hospital ship one night. The next day, I was transferred to a mobile hospital unit on the beach, like a M.A.S.H. unit (Mobile Army Surgical Hospital). There were a lot of men in the hospital, but none from my company. Near the hospital tent was an artillery position; it seemed like it was right next to the hospital tent, and every time it was fired, it felt like I would fly up a foot off the bunk. The firing did not help my ears, either.

When I returned to my company, they were helping in the attack on Cactus Ridge. They were farther south and were now facing the main line of resistance by the Japanese. I reported to the rear supply area, which was set up in a schoolhouse with a courtyard around it. Sgt. Dominic Mondell, the supply sergeant, was here along with the cooks and motor pool drivers. I stayed overnight with them, and the next day, I went with one of the supply trucks to where the company was.

When I reported to the company commander, I was told to stay with the supply personnel until I was healed. My platoon was out on the front line, and there was no way to get me to them, so I returned to the supply area

After I got back to Company B, I learned that Bill Koenecke had been evacuated after being wounded. He had been hit with machine-gun fire in his chest and left arm. I heard later that he had lost his arm and would be going back to a hospital in the States. The company lost a number of other men, too, in addition to Bill.

On April 9th, the 1st and 2nd Battalions, 383rd, were in the proper position to attack Kakazu Ridge. It was to be a day the 383rd would not soon forget.

[9] Kakazu Ridge, E Company, 382d Infantry, rolls forward through heavy enemy fire on the southern front on Okinawa Island. A tank supports infantrymen as they cautiously move forward.

[9] (US National WWII Archives Catalog; 1945)

CHAPTER 6

Kakazu Ridge

The Meatgrinder

Kakazu Ridge was the western flank of a line of ridges running most of the way across the island. Stretching about 1,000 yards, it was separated from the Nishibaru Ridge on the east by a cut and, on the west, sloped down to the sea. In appearance and elevation, Kakazu was not a particularly formidable barrier, but the deep gorges separating it from us could be scaled only with difficulty, and its defenses were something out of this world. The reverse slope was infested with mortars, all zeroed in on the gorge, and the ridge itself was defended by an intricate pattern of pillboxes, tunnels, and caves which covered every possible avenue of approach.

The two assault battalions were ordered to jump off in a surprise attack at 5 a.m., with the 1st Battalion (ours) attacking the main ridge and the 3rd Battalion attacking Kakazu West ridge. The 1st attacked with A Company on the left and C Company on the right. Under cover of predawn darkness, both companies navigated the gorge and, by daylight, had reached the crest of the ridge without being discovered.

Then, a Japanese soldier in a pillbox spotted A Company and opened fire. This was immediately followed by a terrific hail of mortar and artillery fire along the entire regimental front, punctuated by the fire of countless machine guns. Most of the men of our companies had reached the top of the ridge but did not have contact with each other, yet. To make matters worse, their support platoons were now pinned down in the open ground between the gorge and the ridge by the scathing fire from above.

The Japanese, without waiting for their mortar fire to cease, began charging the forward elements of the two companies. Hand-to-hand fighting raged furiously, and Capt. Royster, A Company Commander, reported that his situation was critical. He reported that unless reinforcements could be brought up, he would be forced to withdraw or risk being wiped out. B Company, my company, had been in reserve but was now ordered to move up behind A Company. We were completely pinned down by enemy fire as we tried to cross the open ground north of the gorge.

By 8:30 a.m., A Company's situation had become desperate, and C Company was receiving a strong counterattack on its exposed left flank. The chemical mortar company was having a difficult time laying down smoke because of the strong wind blowing toward the front lines. Without the cover of a smokescreen, neither company was able to withdraw. Finally, at 10 a.m., the smoke was considered effective, and the companies started their withdrawal, a desperate feat in itself.

The wounded were sent first, assisted by a few of the able-bodied men, while the rest continued to fire from the crest to protect their retreat. Finally, the remaining men, plus the elements of the two companies who had been pinned down to the rear in the open ground (not B Company), made their way to the gorge. They were not out of danger, however, as the

Japanese had their mortars zeroed in on the gorge, and concentrations were continually falling in their midst.

At 10:30 a.m., the first members of A and C companies reached the gorge, where they were met by Capt. John Van Vulpen, commander of B Company. Vulpen, along with the forward elements of B Company, had just reached this point in an attempt to reinforce the other two companies. The rest of us in B Company had not made it this far yet.

Capt. Van Vulpen reported the situation to battalion headquarters and was ordered to gather all available men and resume the attack. He totaled the able-bodied men of the three companies who had reached this point and found he had 46 men. He was under orders to attack, so, rallying the weary men, he led them up the south bank of the draw and out into the open.

They had only gone a few yards when they were met by a hail of fire from machine guns and mortars that instantly wounded seven of the men. It was apparent that it was impossible to advance any further, so, fashioning litters from ponchos, they dragged the wounded men back into the ravine where some more of us from B Company joined them.

Being caught in an open area with very little coverage is something you never want to happen. We managed to work our way backward and to the right to finally get around to where Capt. Van Vulpen was. There was a lot of mortar and machine-gun fire all around us, and we lost more men during our withdrawal. What we wanted was just to get out of there and for the firing to stop.

The captain decided that we had to find a way to get the men out of the gorge, where they were still suffering from mortar and artillery fire from the enemy. Lt. William Neiman, B Company 4th platoon leader, led a small group of men armed with two light machine guns and formed the point of an escape party that started to work its way northwest up the ravine toward the 3rd Battalion lines. As we came under heavy fire, this leading unit became split off from the main body.

Capt. Van Vulpen decided that a litter squad was needed and that the withdrawal was impossible without the aid of smoke. The company's only radio (I didn't have one that day) had been left behind in the open during the last futile attack, so the captain told Lt. Leo Ford to take command of the men while he and Sgt. John Summers made their way back to the battalion to get fire support and arrange for the evacuation of the wounded.

Lt. Neiman and his small group finally made it to the 3rd Battalion lines about dusk on their own. Meanwhile, Capt. Van Vulpen and Sgt. Summers ran the gauntlet back to the battalion command post. Their trip was a nightmare of hairbreadth escapes, and both men were completely unnerved by the time they arrived and in no condition to lead the rescue party back.

Sgt. William McEhleran, a communications sergeant, led a volunteer group of twelve men with litters back into the gully. Only eight of them made it. Knowing the need for the smoke to cover their withdrawal, Sgt. McEhleran and Pfc. Charles Bassett crawled back to the fire-swept ground where the attack had halted and recovered the radio. Lt. Ford contacted the battalion command post and pleaded for the smoke.

There was little of this ammunition left, but Capt. Hugh Young, the battalion S-3, collected all that could be rounded up. Lt. Ford attempted to adjust the rounds, but every time he would rise up to look, the Japanese would fire on him. Finally, Capt. Young was firing almost entirely by map. And then the supply of smoke ammunition ran out. We learned later that when Capt. Young informed Lt. Ford there would be no more smoke; he also told him, "God help you, Leo." Nobody thought we would be coming back.

When Lt. Ford got the word that there was no more smoke, he knew we didn't have any other option but to try to find our way out under cover of the inadequate smoke we had. By 4 p.m., we had inched our way to a point in a ravine across from the north slope of Kakazu West. We were all shaken and wondering how long this was going to last.

Suddenly, planes appeared, and we almost cheered because we thought they would hit the Japanese positions and we would be able to complete our withdrawal. Somebody erred, though, and the airstrike was almost right on top of us. Although none of us were hit, the explosions loosed large rocks and boulders, showering them down on us and forcing us to take cover in caves.

When the airstrike was over, Lt. Ford almost had to force us to leave the caves. I think most of us knew that if we stayed there, the Japanese would infiltrate the area after dark, and many of us would die. Lt. Ford had us split into little groups of three and four men, and then each group began to work its way toward our lines. Some of the men made it back before dark, but most of us came back after dark. Seven men didn't return until the next morning, four of them walking and the other three crawling.

You didn't know who or what you were going to meet when you came around a large boulder. Sometimes, you had to crawl to keep from being seen, and sometimes, you just ran across an open area, hoping you would make it.

The "lost battalion," 1st Battalion, 383rd, lost fifty percent of its men at Kakazu Ridge that day. The 383rd Regiment had 386 casualties. The three attack companies had 15 dead, 73 missing and presumed dead, and 50 more wounded. With so many casualties and the intensity of the enemy fire, I still wonder how Brower, Mandel, Spellazza, and I made it through that day without being wounded.

# # #

The military newspaper *Stars and Stripes* had a reporter, Pfc. Williams Land, assigned to the 96th Infantry. Land filed this story from the battle for Kakazu Ridge.

("Stars and Stripes presents these archive reports as they were written by the reporters in the field. The graphic and politically incorrect language used may be offensive to some readers.")

WITH 96th DIV. OKINAWA (Delayed) — A bunch of doughfeet of an infantry regiment were hanging around, not doing much of anything. Some were lining their foxholes with paper boxes to hold back the moisture. Others were eating K-rations, or just talking.

The 12 men were all that were left of a rifle platoon, after days of battle against strong Jap fortifications on Kakazu Ridge, the "Siegfried Line" of Okinawa.

Only the day before, they had repulsed a terrific counterattack by a well-armed and well-equipped Japanese company.

It was a battle of 12 against 150.

Stiff Resistance

At the beginning of the campaign, the going had been easy, with advance over the comparatively flat terrain fairly rapid. Then on Kakazu Ridge, the Japs gave our troops the stiffest resistance yet encountered in the battle for Oki. The men had to stop and dig in. They lay there for two days and night in cold and rain, while the Japs sat comfortably in their deep caves throwing "flying boxcars" at them.

"A flying boxcar is a 220mm spigot mortar shell which looks something like a 50-gallon drum," explained Pfc. Marvin E. McDonald of Cle Elum, Wash., a rifleman in the platoon.

"You see those things come down on you, looming up as big as the side of a barn. On contact with the ground they burst like an overripe watermelon, causing a terrific concussion and a hail of falling rocks."

Order To Attack

At 0530 on the third day, the order came to attack a well-protected row of foxholes only about 150 yards ahead.

Under a rain of machine gun bullets and mortar shells they made a dash over the rocks and through the heavy underbrush, diving into the foxholes.

Soon thereafter all hell broke loose, and the Jap counterattack began.

Pfc. Walter Aklin, Hamlin, Tex., was the first to notice six Jap helmets moving toward their foxholes and yelled a warning to the other men. Everybody opened up.

Kills Six Japs

Aklin's BAR failed. He began disassembling it under fire. The recoil spring was weak and wouldn't feed to the chamber. Stretching the spring, he slapped the parts together again. Then he emptied two magazines of bullets into the advancing Japs. A second later, the six were lying dead almost on the embankment of his foxhole.

"One of them was virtually cut in half," he said.

For a while everything was quiet. The platoon's supply of ammunition was low. Frantically they looked through their packs for extra grenades. Then the Japs started up again with the mortars and big rocks. It was now obvious that everything was directed to one spot. All hit within 15 feet of Aklin's and Purdlebough's foxhole.

Later they saw that they'd been lying right next to a big hole filled with dynamite and picric acid stored by the Japs.

"If they'd hit the dump," said Purdlebough, "the whole squad would have been blown to bits."

Nips Swarm All Over

Suddenly the Japs swarmed all over them. They appeared from behind rocks and hidden caves, setting up knee-mortars and throwing grenades. In front, a Jap officer flourished a sword, egging his men on with loud yells. Purdlebough finished him off, while the others opened up with their last ammunition, virtually mowing down the Nips.

The rest of the Japs fled and, hiding behind rock and trees, started to roll grenades down the hill toward the doughboys' foxholes. They were kept pinned down, however.

In the meantime the heavy weapons company moved in and began setting up mortars. Sgt. Purdlebough directed the fire.

Shells Come Closer

The first shells hit 75 yards behind the enemy line: Purdlebough hollered for closer range.

The Japs were finished and knew it. The few left tried to get back into their caves, but were killed with their own grenades, which they had left behind.

After the battle, the count was 150 "good" Japs.

This morning, the rest of E Company was relieved from frontline duty and is now guarding an airstrip and part of the coast against paratroop and amphibious landings.

The boys are calling it a rest. [10]

# # #

---

[10] (Land, Williams, Pfc. Stars and Stripes Archives, 1945)

Colonel King, 1st Battalion commander, was convinced the battalion would be wiped out if we didn't withdraw. When he conveyed this to regimental headquarters, he was told reinforcements were on the way, and, to hold his position. When he continued to protest, Colonel May relieved him of his command, and Major Kenny Erickson succeeded him.

The order came down, "Renew the attack," but on April 11th, when the attack was renewed, the 1st Battalion was in reserve because it had suffered so many casualties on the 9th. The 2nd and 3rd Battalions, 383rd, and the 381st were the lead units on this new push to take Kakazu Ridge and Kakazu West.

However, on the night of the 12th, the Japanese threw everything they had at us, trying to push us back off the ground we held. We all had to fight to the best of our abilities to stop the attack. A force of about 60 Japanese attacked G Company and nearly broke through because our men had thought they were friendly troops coming back. However, they worked fast when they realized the truth, and in the morning, 58 bodies were lying in front of their position. We turned back an attack in our zone with a count of 20 dead Japanese, and none of us lost.

This was also the day we learned that President Franklin D. Roosevelt had died, and Harry S Truman was our new Commander-in-Chief. We were all saddened by this news, but we had seen so many of our friends die, and we were kind of hardened to this type of news. I guess the only way we could honor FDR was by continuing the fight for the freedom of all people. I think there were probably memorial services held back in the rear echelons.

Our Division was relieved the next day by elements of the 27th Infantry Division. Technically, we had failed in our mission, but it could not have been any other way, considering the forces we had faced, the terrain, and the way they were dug in. The battle for Kakazu will stand as one of the proudest, even if tragic, moments on our road to victory.

Our efforts had not been in vain. When Kakazu finally fell on April 24th, over 600 Japanese bodies were found in a common grave. The 383rd, now a mere shell of itself, was moved to the rear.

We moved into the rear area, set up our tents, dug foxholes on the perimeter, and set up mess tents and a supply tent. 1st Sgt. Gerstner had me report to the supply tent because Sgt. Mondell had asked for my assistance during this period of being re-supplied with equipment and men. *(I even got to sleep on a cot in the supply tent!)*

We were supplied with a generator that provided lights for the mess tent, supply tent, and company headquarters tent. We also had to dig foxholes outside the supply tent in case of an air raid or incoming artillery.

When the wires from the generator were strung to the supply tent, they put them up on poles. I told Sgt. Mondell that the lines were too low, but he said they would be okay for the short time we would be there. To make a long story short, we had an air raid warning late one afternoon. We all dashed from the supply tent to the foxholes; I made it to mine okay, but I thought Sgt. Mondell was going to hang himself when he hit that power line with his head. His helmet went flying, and his feet went out from under him, and he landed flat on his back. Thankfully, only his dignity was hurt. Needless to say, the lines were higher the next day.

One other night, the men on the perimeter pulling guard duty shot a carabao cow that was roaming around in the dark. Our cooks butchered it, and we had fresh meat to eat. I think the men on guard duty knew it was a cow all the time.

On April 19th, our Division was again sent forward. This time, we were not in the Kakazu Ridge zone. The 381st and 382nd Regiments were the lead attack forces, with the 383rd in reserve. The 1st Battalion of the 383rd had been pretty well shot up, and we were still trying to get more replacements.

The Japanese were savagely fighting to keep the Division from capturing Nishibaru Ridge and the town of Nishibaru. On the 21st, the 3rd Battalion, 383rd, was attached to the 382nd to help them in the effort to take Hill 7 and move on to Table Rock, but almost immediately, the battalion ran into trouble from a small hill that the 382nd had occupied the day before. It seems some Japanese had played possum, as the 3rd Battalion now found themselves under fire from several machine guns, and later that day we were hit by a heavy mortar barrage. We made little progress that day.

On April 22nd, the 2nd Battalion, 383rd completed the relief of the 382nd Regiment, which had been online for 19 days. The

2nd Battalion of the 382nd remained on the line with the 3rd Battalion of the 383rd, because they were less cut up than the other two battalions. They were under orders to remain in position until Kakazu Ridge was disposed of by a coordinated attack with the 7th Division on April 24th.

[11] A 37mm anti-tank gun prepares to fire point-blank at a Japanese pillbox on Conical Hill on Okinawa. The 383rd Infantry Regiment of the Army's 96th Infantry Division found this small weapon effective.

[11] (US Army Archives, Wikipedia Commons, 1945)

CHAPTER 7

More Hills to Claim

Easy, Fox, Charlie, King, and Conical

On April 19th, we moved up into the hills behind the attacking forces and were ready to support any of the other battalions as needed. As our forces advanced, we would move to another hill and dig in. After our troops took Hill 150 and Hill 152, we moved onto a hill to their rear in the 382nd's zone of attack.

I was a part of company headquarters now, and we were positioned in a log bunker on the crest of the hill. The platoons were in foxholes on both the forward and reverse slopes of the hill. From our position on the crest of the hill, we could see the movement of the Japanese on the hill across the valley in front of us. One day, Sgt. Elmer Sweeter set up his light machine gun about 50 feet in front of our CP and waited for movement on the opposite hill.

The Japanese must have had a series of bunkers across the face of the hill, and, every so often, we would see a Japanese soldier run up the hill from one bunker to the next. They seemed to be carrying something as they ran. Elmer watched and adjusted his weapon for the range, and, when the Japanese soldier came out of the bunker, he would open fire. He shot a number of them before they quit trying to make the run between the bunkers. We would see a puff of smoke when they were hit, and, we thought they were probably carrying ammo of some kind.

One day while we were in reserve and it was relatively quiet, one of the other men and I decided to explore the hill beneath us. In our bunker, there was a small hole about two feet in diameter with a wooden ladder down into it. We went down the ladder and found a long room at the bottom. There were wooden tables and benches in the room, as well as mats for sleeping. At the far end was another opening and another long room like the first one. There was another hole in this room with another ladder, and we found another floor of rooms below and another floor below that one. Three floors of rooms were dug down into the hill we were camped on. We found many hills fortified like this as we moved further ahead.

We were under attack by Japanese artillery fire while we were on this hill. It seemed the Japanese had zeroed their artillery in on the reverse slope of our hill before we had taken it, and now, when they fired at us, the rounds were going over us and landing in our rear. The rounds were just barely getting over the crest of the hill — we had to stay down to avoid being hit. One night, we heard one shell hit the hill, and we waited for the explosion, but it never came. In the morning, we found the shell sticking out of the dirt on top of the bunker. Ordinance men came and removed it for us. Another time, we counted eleven shells going over us that landed in the valley behind us, and each one was a dud. The twelfth shell exploded.

This was also where we heard and saw the results of a 150-mm cannon. The shell would be propelled up a chute, and when it left the chute, it would tumble end-over-end as it flew, making a loud, screaming sound. There was no missing its approach! We only had one shot at us and it went over us, landing in the valley behind, creating a hole big enough for a two-and-a-half-ton truck. We kept getting replacements while we were here, and though we never did get to full strength again, we got enough to help us operate as a company again. One day, we heard a shot in our area, and when we checked it out, we found one of the new men had shot his foot. He said it was an accident, but most of us thought he did it on purpose. We heard rumors of ways to do this without getting crippled, but if this guy did it on purpose, he did a poor job of it because the medics said he would be crippled for the rest of his life.

We had a replacement lieutenant who carried a pair of pearl-handled revolvers, trying to be like General Patton, I guess. I came by his foxhole one day, and he was sitting on the edge of the hole working with a file. He said he was filing the deep grooves in the head of each bullet, so if it hit an enemy, it would split and make a bigger hole. I don't know if this ever worked or not because he was wounded the next time we went online.

("I think I must have matured some while I was in the hospital and working in the supply area because as I am writing this, I have been trying to think of who led the work parties that went down to the bottom of the hills and carried up the ammunition, rations, and water which the trucks would bring to us. And then I realized it was ME. I was the one who had been asked to do it by 1st Sgt. Gerstner." —JWZ, 2004)

We continued to get replacements, and they received intensive training. Some of the best training they received, however, was during the bull sessions with the men in their squads and platoons. We all knew we needed these men to achieve our objective, so there wasn't any problem getting them integrated into their squads.

On April 30th the last elements of the 383rd were relieved by elements of the 77th Division. The 383rd, heavily dependent on the young replacements, had driven a dagger to the very core of the Japanese defenders.

In the few days available for rest, the recreation services of the Division moved into high gear. The Division Band members put aside their rifles and played for fourteen shows.

While we were still on the line, the premiere of the movie "Wilson" was shown. The movie was halted nine times by the wail of air raid sirens, but the men wanted to see it and kept coming back.

After we were relieved, we moved to another area in the rear and set up our tents. The American Red Cross set up a tent in our battalion area, complete with several Red Cross workers. It was nice to be able to go there to play cards, write letters (they furnished the paper), play table tennis, and participate in parlor games. Some of us went for no other reason than to talk to a woman, for most of the workers were women.

("My Division history book says that during combat, the Red Cross and regimental service companies teamed up to bring coffee and doughnuts to the front lines. I don't remember getting any of it!!" —JWZ, 2004)

Soon after, on May 9th, the word of the victory in Europe came to us as we were moving back to the front lines to relieve the 7th Division. I don't think we will forget that VE-Day. It was a miserable day. The roads were ankle-deep in mud, and we moved silently and slowly toward the front and the war, the war that was just beginning for many soldiers. It may sound callous, but VE-Day was very far away and unimportant to us that day.

VE-Day coincided with the start of the rainy season (monsoons), and we continued to have rain nearly every day. The roads got so bad the supply vehicles did not make it through to us every day. Pvt. Francis (Red) Beeler, a jeep driver, was the one who made it up to the company the most times. He would stand up and lean back against the seat, push down on the gas pedal, and go as fast as he could. Sometimes, you could hardly see the wheels because the mud was so deep.

("The only reason Red was a private was because he was always doing something that resulted in him losing his private first-class stripe. I think if he had behaved, he could have made at least corporal." —JWZ, 2004)

One morning, Red came roaring up the road through the mud, and we could hear him yelling as he came. It seems the cooks had come up with a brilliant idea: bake loaves of bread for the guys on the front lines! They did, and Red was delivering it. We didn't have any butter, but, boy, did that bread taste good! After that, maybe in part because of our enthusiastic reaction to the fresh bread, we would occasionally get more.

On May 11th, there was to be a four-division attack, with the 96th on the left, the 77th Division on the right, and the 1st and 6th Marine Divisions beyond them. The 96th was ordered to take the high ground guarding Shuri from the north and east, seize Conical Hill, the eastern anchor of the Shuri line, and then take the high ground to its south. The main effort was to be with the 382nd against the Shuri line and the 383rd to attack Conical Hill.

The day before the scheduled attack, May 10th, we moved into position on the east slope of Easy Hill. Our main thrust was to take a series of smaller hills — bearing our code names: Easy, Fox, Charlie, and King — which led from the north onto Conical's western slopes. The 2nd Battalion was to strike south across the coastal flatlands from Gaja Ridge.

Major Erickson, Battalion Commander, gave B Company the job of capturing Easy Hill. Thanks largely to the efforts of Pfc. (later Sgt.) Ben Tlougan this was accomplished in short order. The Japanese had good positions on the peak of the hill and threw grenades down on the climbing men, but Ben moved ahead of his platoon, stood in the open, and fired twenty or thirty grenades of his own at the defenders. He couldn't carry that many by himself, so the other men in the platoon were passing their grenades up to him. After he had killed several Japanese, the rest fled, and the company moved up to the crest.

I was with company headquarters now and was at the company command post when this happened. One of my jobs at company headquarters was preparing the daily morning report and casualty report that was sent to battalion headquarters. Along with the reports, he also asked me to write up the recommendations for the awarding of medals.

(Sgt. Gerstner had discovered my handwriting was decipherable by other people.)

Word of Ben's heroics spread quickly, and 1st Sgt. Gerstner asked me to write up what Ben had done so it could be sent up the chain of command recommending him for a Bronze Star Medal. After it reached regimental headquarters, it was apparently changed because he received the Silver Star Medal. Unfortunately, he received it posthumously, as Ben was killed three days after his heroic actions.

The same day we secured Easy Hill we also secured Fox Hill, which had been defended by twenty or thirty Japanese. Lt. Sam Hilton was a replacement officer who had joined the company the afternoon before. During the attempt to secure the hill, we came under artillery and mortar fire from the Japanese, and he was killed by shrapnel. Such a short time to be with us. We never even got to know him. But even with his death, we were off to a good start.

After Easy Hill was secured, I took three other men and two litters and went through a series of trenches the Japanese had dug on the Hill to bring back two of our men who had been wounded. It was a little harrowing because the trenches were only about four feet deep, which left us exposed to fire from Japanese rifles and machine guns. There were some sharp turns in the trenches, and at each one, we had to lift the litter to get them around the turn. It also meant that we had to stand up, too. We made it back without getting hit, and I wrote up the other three men for the Bronze Star Medal, which they all received.

(Nobody wrote me up that I knew about, but after the war, I was notified of being awarded the medal.)

We were bombarded with artillery and mortar fire every day while we were on this hill. It caused one of our men to go almost crazy. Each time there was a bombardment, the men would jump into their foxholes to try to be safe. Three times when this happened, this man had a foxhole buddy killed in his hole, and he didn't even get a scratch. I guess he was starting to think he was a jinx. The fourth time it happened, he received a shrapnel wound in the buttocks. We had never seen someone so happy to be wounded!

("Poor guy was from St. Paul. He made it through the rest of the war, but shortly after I returned home in 1946, I read in the St. Paul newspaper that his car had been struck by a train, and he was killed." —JWZ, 2004)

While we were still dug in on Easy, we received some sniper fire from our left flank, so Capt. Van Vulpen decided to send out a patrol to look for the sniper. I went along as the radioman, and we moved out over the flatlands and into the low hills. I don't recall finding the sniper, but when we realized we were not going to get back to our company before dark, we moved into the nearby city of Yonabaru. The city was the 3rd largest city of Okinawa, with a population of about 25,000, and all we could see was rubble. As far as we could see, there was only one building standing: a train depot. I don't remember how we got on top of the depot, but that's where our patrol stayed the night. We set up a light machine gun and posted guards. We had C rations with us for food and canteens of water. The next morning, we made our way back to our company.

Late in the afternoon of May 12th, the 2nd Battalion, 381st, was sent up to guard the left flank, and G Company moved onto Conical Hill's eastern spur next to our positions. Usually, when we were on the front lines, we had a forward observer team from the artillery with us. The line companies appreciated the observer teams because they could direct artillery fire where we needed it very quickly. However, during the move, which was under heavy fire, a forward observer from the 361st Field Artillery was killed, and Capt. Louis Reuter, G Company commander, was seriously wounded.

A considerable gap now existed between the 1st Battalion and the 2nd. General Bradley wanted this hole plugged, so Colonel May ordered the 3rd Battalion to send one company to do this. Company L drew this assignment, and on the evening of the 12th, they moved up to the base of King Hill and dug in. A twenty- to thirty-yard gap still existed, but machine guns were set up to cover this potential route of infiltration.

On May 13th, while the 2nd Battalion was trying to attack and secure Conical Hill, we were trying to advance up Charlie Hill. Our company managed to reach the top and killed 25 to 30 Japanese on the reverse slope, but their machine gun and mortar fire were taking a devastating toll on us. When T/Sgt. Donald Scott found himself with only six able-bodied men left, he ordered a withdrawal. Four of our men had been killed, and sixteen were wounded, including the platoon leader, Lt. Wm. Neiman.

The Japanese had counted too heavily on the natural strength of their position on the eastern spur and had not committed enough of their forces to defend it. On the 13th, the deciding blow to the Japanese came when two platoon leaders of F Company, without waiting for orders, raced their men to the top. When the Japanese attacked, F Company was already dug in and ready for them. The loss of Conical's eastern spur was a blow from which the Japanese never recovered.

No further moves could be made on Conical Hill while the 1st Battalion was on the north slope of Charlie Hill. We still needed to take Charlie, King, and Love Hills. On the 14th, the three companies of the 1st Battalion tried to take control of Charlie Hill. B Company, my company, tried to move over the top of the hill but got nowhere. A and C Companies, though, hit the flanks, made important gains, and by day's end, our lines formed a wide U around Charlie Hill.

That evening, our company CP was set up in a burial tomb that had been cut into the hillside. The opening to the tomb was about three feet high and two feet wide. There were steps cut out of the back wall on which urns were set, urns that held the bones of the deceased. The inside of the tomb was probably about 10 feet wide, eight feet deep, and seven feet high. There was a courtyard in front of the tomb, with a low stone wall around it. This courtyard was probably about twelve feet square. There was also about 20 to 30 feet of earth above the opening to the tomb. We moved the urns outside in the courtyard against the base of the hill and moved our CP in.

That night, the company commander, executive officer, 1st sergeant, communications sergeant, and the commander's radioman stayed in the tomb. The two telephone wiremen dug a foxhole in the right corner of the courtyard, and I dug my foxhole in the left corner. Everything was fine. We had good cover; the three of us in the courtyard would take turns at guard duty, and the others could get some much-needed rest. Then, sometime during the night, we came under Japanese artillery and mortar fire, waking us up. A couple of rounds exploded on the hill above the tomb.

And then it happened!!

We were all hunkered down in our foxholes, the two wiremen in theirs and me alone in mine when suddenly I heard a voice say, "Wes, get out of your foxhole!" I hesitated and heard the voice say it again, "Wes, get out of your foxhole!" and this time, the voice also said, "Get into the tomb!" Grabbing my rifle, I ran to the tomb and dove into the opening. Just as I went through, I heard the explosion of another shell. The men in the tomb made room for me, and I spent the rest of the night there. I asked who had called my name and warned me to leave my foxhole, but no one had.

In the morning, after shoveling dirt away from the opening, the first thing we saw when we came out of the tomb was my foxhole. My nice square foxhole was now a round hole about twice the size it had been. A shell had made a direct hit. Captain Van Vulpen looked at the hole and said, "Zimmy, Somebody up there likes you." and everyone agreed.

Later when I thought about this, I realized that nobody in the company ever called me "Wes." It was always Zimmy or Jake. Only my mother called me Wes. And God! God is with us wherever we go!

(Reader, I want you to understand. I believe in God and Jesus Christ, His Son. I believe God has the power to perform miracles and, if He so desires, to talk to us. I was baptized and admitted to the Methodist Episcopal Church in April 1938 and have been a member and a worker ever since.

In January 1944, while at Fort Snelling for my pre-induction physical examination, four of us Jackson draftees, Wendell Brown, Harold Bute, Orville Stofferan, and I went to a Baptist mission servicemen's club in the basement of a house just outside the gate to the fort. That night, I accepted the Lord Jesus Christ as my Savior, and I still do today. Wendell knew of this club because he was a member of the Baptist Church.)

We stayed in these positions for two weeks, sending out patrols every day trying to find a way to get over this hill and on to the next. We called in airstrikes and artillery fire on King Hill, but every time the bombardment was lifted the Japanese were right there with their artillery, mortars, and machine guns to keep us from advancing.

We later learned the Japanese had caves on the forward slope of King Hill and had artillery pieces inside installed on tracks. Whenever we called for artillery or airstrikes, they could quickly pull their weapons back on the tracks, safe in the shelter of the caves, and as soon as we stopped, they would bring them out again. We tried sending demolition men with the patrols so they could try to demolish the entrances to the caves. We succeeded with some, but not enough.

On May 16th, our battalion commander, Major Kenny Erickson, was wounded during a mortar barrage, and Capt. Hugh Young assumed command. Our objective that day was Love Hill, which, if secured, would give us an approach to Conical Hill, as well as afford support for the 382nd's attack on Oboe Hill. C Company, which was also on Charlie Hill, was selected for this assault. The direct assault was made by the 2nd Platoon, and when their support units ran into immediate trouble, the 26 men were completely alone when they moved out. To make matters worse, they still had the enemy to their rear.

The Japanese allowed them to get partway up the hill, but as they approached the crest, they were hit by the most murderous concentration of machine-gun fire we had ever seen. It was estimated that at least 50 machine guns had been firing on them from Charlie, King, Conical, Love, and Oboe Hills. Helpless to aid them, we could only look on in horror as one man after another staggered and fell. To those of us watching, it appeared every man had been killed.

There were, however, a few who survived, including the platoon sergeant. At eight o'clock that night, under cover of darkness, he and five other soldiers made their way back to our lines. Four had been wounded in the initial attack on the hill, and the other two were hit on the way back.

Four days later, early in the morning, as a flare went up, riflemen on the perimeter saw two figures waving and calling to us not to shoot. Keeping them covered, we watched them until they were close enough for us to recognize them as American soldiers. One of them went back and brought in two others, and a little later, a fifth man came staggering in. They had survived three days and nights by staying in a tomb at the bottom of the hill. They survived American artillery fire and machine-gun fire. On the third night, when one of them slipped out of the tomb to a shell hole to get some water, he saw a fire in front of a cave and heard the Japanese singing and having a party. He also heard women's voices there. When he told the others, they decided it was now or never. Leaving all their equipment, they even removed their shoes to prevent making any noise, and successfully slipped out of the tomb and made their way back to us.

All of them were in pitiful condition and tired beyond exhaustion. They were covered with flea bites, their eyes were sunken, and their cheeks were drawn. None of the men had slept a wink, because the fleas made that impossible.

(We always had to check each other for fleas when we stayed in tombs.)

Before they were sent to the rear, they were able to give us information about the positions of the Japanese mortars and machine guns. The two wounded men were immediately hospitalized, and the other three were sent to bed. A few days later those three were back on the lines.

With our continued patrols pushing at the Japanese defenses, we now held all of Charlie Hill except for the draw between its southeast and southwest fingers. We were not able to gain control of this area until the Japanese withdrew two weeks later. Our whole battalion was drastically weakened and the loss of experienced personnel had reached a grave point. Almost every man in the battalion had seen the slaughter of C Company's 2nd Platoon the day before.

As of May 20th, more than 300 men had been killed or wounded in the battle to take Charlie Hill. The pocket of Japanese on the rear slope was holding up the advance of the entire regiment, and tanks and infantry seemed equally helpless to do anything about it.

An airstrike against Charlie was not considered practical because the bombs would have to land within 100 yards of our lines. It would also be necessary to run the strike backward toward our lines to get at the pocket. However, Lt. Charles (Red) Hymers of the 383rd Reconnaissance Platoon had been observing the terrain daily from a Piper Cub plane and convinced the regimental commander it could be done because he knew the area so thoroughly; he could guide the striking planes to the exact spot.

The Japanese force on the rear slope was small enough that it was deemed safe to withdraw us from Charlie Hill long enough for the strike to be run. Four Marine torpedo bombers and eight carrier-based Navy planes made the strike, with Lt. Hymers riding in the lead Marine bomber pointing out the precise targets to the pilot. The planes flew at an altitude of 15 feet, dropped their 500-pound bombs, and zoomed up almost vertically to avoid crashing into the hill.

Back we came, and it was the same old story! Capt. Van Vulpen led two platoons through the cut, and before they could get back under the smokescreen several hours later, five men had been wounded, and four men were missing. Company A had no better luck trying to go over the crest. They were stopped by enemy fire from Love Hill. It had been a well-conceived and executed plan, but it just didn't work.

On the 21st, Love Hill was again the objective, and again, C Company was hit by fire from three directions as it reached the base. We had reached Charlie Hill on May 11th, and, as night fell on the 21st, we were still there. It was clear that our continual pressure was taking its toll on the Japanese defenders. All along the line, we were making deeper penetrations into their positions.

The rains had increased to a steady downpour. It soon became clear that we wouldn't be able to continue our progress under those conditions. On May 22nd, the advance of the entire Tenth Army ground to a halt. Roads became impassable. Even the "weasel," an M-29 cargo carrier that had been used with success on Leyte, was powerless to push its way through the thick adhesive clay which clung to its tracks and clogged up the suspension system until it choked out the motor. The clinging mud strained the engines of all vehicles to the limits of their power and beyond. The roads were lined with vehicles whose cooling systems had given up the struggle.

Food, ammunition, and water were carried on the straining backs of hundreds of weary G.I.'s, slipping, sliding, and sinking halfway to their knees, covered from head to foot with caked mud, their clothing soaked with the rain that never stopped. I led a party of men to the base of our hill so we could carry supplies up to our position. We struggled to get back up the hill. When we brought up the last of it, one of the men handed me a canteen cup filled with orangeade, or, so I thought. They had been making a five-gallon can of it, using the packets we received in our C rations. What I didn't know was that someone had also poured some 190-proof alcohol into it. That first swallow burned all the way down! I went and found some water to drink and then made myself a cup of coffee.

("I think if I would have had that when I had hookworm, I wouldn't have had to worry about the hookworm. That was all I took was one swallow of that, and I went and found a can that they didn't have that stuff in." —JWZ, 2004)

There could be no patrols forward of the front lines. Plans were drawn up and attack orders were issued several times between the 22nd to the 25th, but each time the orders were canceled. Lt. Col. Howard Cornutt, the assistant Division G-3, summed it up this way, "Those on the forward slopes slid down. Those on the reverse slopes slid back. Otherwise, no change."

Company A made one last attack on Love Hill on the 23rd. The story was sadly identical to those of the previous days — one man was killed, and 12 were listed as missing. It was more than one platoon leader could stand — he went out of his head and, recklessly exposing himself, was instantly killed.

On the 26th there were indications that the Japanese may be vacating their positions. Reconnaissance reported a lot of movement to the south but hesitated to give it too much importance because there was also some movement north. Our patrols were still encountering stiff resistance from the Japanese. It later became clear that what the patrols encountered was a mere shell of a defense, consisting of well-placed mortars and machine guns supported by a thin line of infantry. On the 29th, we saw the sun again for the first time in ten days. It proved prophetic, for one day later, the Shuri Line collapsed.

On May 30th, we launched a full-scale attack to try to gain control of these hills. It was almost like being out for a Sunday stroll. These hills had been spitting death from every crevasse for three weeks, and now there was hardly anything to stop us. The 381st Regiment made the primary effort and quickly captured Sugar and Cutaway Hills and found them littered with Japanese bodies. By noon, they had captured three more hills against very weak forces and had moved on to a fourth hill.

The Japanese made one last futile gesture in our area. They left a suicide detachment in the Charlie Hill pocket, which the 2nd Battalion quickly disposed of and, by 10 o'clock, had taken Love Hill. They encountered very little resistance as they went on and took four more hills during the day.

The 3rd Battalion also advanced against slight opposition. Their most notable feat was one man personally accounting for several Japanese in a cave.

The 1st Battalion was in reserve that day, and we had a hard time keeping up with the other battalions. When we moved over to Charlie Hill, we could see the caves that had held us up. Close inspection showed they were dug deep into the hillside and had tracks for the artillery pieces to move on. We could see why the airstrikes didn't seem to bother them. Our overall advance that day was 1200 yards, over hills and through valleys.

On May 31st, all units of the 96th swiftly secured all remaining objectives assigned to them. A command decision had been made, and the 96th Division took over the area where the 77th Division had been and extended our area to the southeast corner of Shuri.

The 383rd literally walked into Shuri, the 2nd largest city of Okinawa, looked over the rubble of that once beautiful town, and compared notes with the Marines who had come into the town from the other side. When the Japanese lost Shuri, they lost the battle for Okinawa. Over 2,000 men from our Division were killed in this three-week-long battle, but the Japanese had lost over four times that many, over 8,500 in all. The ground the defenders of Shuri had vowed to never give up was now in our hands.

[12] Silhouetted against the entrance to one of the caves that honeycomb the Okinawa hills, an American rifleman resorts to cat-and-mouse tactics to pick off enemy snipers in the surrounding ridges.

[12] (US Military Archives; American sniper in cave on Okinawa)

CHAPTER 8

Cleaning Up

A Dirty Job

With the fall of Shuri, an enemy not as fanatical as the Japanese would have realized the end was near and would have surrendered. The Japanese were operating under orders to fight until not a man was left, and they intended to do so.

Our Division was pretty beat up from the last three weeks, and if a fresh division had been available, we would have been relieved from combat duty. But as there was nobody to take our place, it again became our duty to take on the job of reducing the main Japanese positions.

The main body of the Japanese had pulled back to the southern end of the island. From June 1st to June 6th, we moved quickly southward against gradually increasing resistance, moving at a rate of about a thousand yards a day.

On one of these days, we came to a cut in a hill. While we were taking a break, a company of Marines passed us. A couple of Marines were carrying a machine gun, but we didn't see any ammunition bearers. When we asked about their ammo bearers, they told us they hadn't seen them for several days. What do you do with a machine gun in battle without any ammunition?

After our break, we moved up to the cut. The Marines were there, trying to get through. One man at a time would go through the cut, and each time, a Japanese sniper would shoot him. We waited and watched for a time, and then Capt. Van Vulpen told the Marine officer to hold his men back, and we would try to get through. He ordered us to go single file, run through the cut, and then dive into the cover on the other side. We did this, and as soon as several were through, they went out and got the sniper.

Richard Miller wore glasses because he was far-sighted. He had broken his glasses on Leyte, and we discovered he was a crack shot without them. He was the designated sniper in our company, and he was the one who got the Japanese sniper who had been delaying the Marines.

Later that day, after another skirmish with a small Japanese group, I spotted something in a helmet by a dead man, and, picking the helmet up, I found a Japanese family flag folded up and placed inside the helmet. I still have that flag today. Some of our men picked up pistols, rifles, and swords, but I knew I would have a hard time taking something like that home with me. If the Japanese soldier had not been recently killed, I would not have touched anything because, given time, the Japanese would rig booby traps on their dead soldiers.

On June 3rd, we started to run into some trouble on our right flank because the Marines had trouble with a pocket of stiff resistance south of Naha and could not keep up with our swift advance southward. We continued to move forward rapidly and took a heavy toll on over 100 Japanese as they tried to run from us.

Behind us, our forces sent demolition teams to search the caves in the hills. They would come up to a cave entrance and use a loudspeaker to call into the cave and tell anyone in the cave to come out. If no one came out in a reasonable amount of time, they would set charges of explosives around the entrance and blow it shut. This netted very few Japanese soldiers, but numerous civilians came out, sometimes as many as 300. After Okinawa was secured, we heard of many civilians being rescued from some of the blown-shut caves because someone heard voices in them, and the Army had to use heavy equipment to open the caves up.

The weather continued to be rainy all this time, and supplies were getting critically low. The north/south highway had been washed out north of Yonabaru, so supplies and casualties were received by water from that port. The road south of Yonabaru was terrible, too, prompting an airdrop of supplies to us on June 3rd, but the supplies landed in the Marine sector. (Well, maybe they needed the ammunition *so they could get that machine gun working again!)*

On the 4th, the Japanese resistance increased, but the front moved forward almost another mile. The Marines were still heavily engaged to the rear, so the boundaries were readjusted to bring the Yaeju Dake Hill mass into the 96th zone of action.

On the morning of the 5th, the road-junction town of Iwa fell to the 2nd Battalion. It was full of natives, and our men captured a few soldiers in civilian clothes. The 1st Battalion, 381st, had captured five hills and killed 55 Japanese spotted digging in on another hill. We all moved as much as a mile that day, but the loss of another gallant soldier overshadowed the day's progress. A Japanese machine gunner had put a bullet through the heart of Col. Edwin T. May, our regimental commander, while he was directing the fight from a forward observation post as he always did. A posthumous award of the Distinguished Service Cross recognized his leadership ability. Lt. Col. DeWitt Ballard, regimental executive officer, now assumed command of the 383rd.

Looming less than a thousand yards ahead was a sight we all remembered: Sawtooth Ridge, which we had been able to see from Charlie Hill. We just knew this was where the Japanese would make their last stand. The obstacle that faced us was a steep V-shaped ridge, open on the north and anchored on two rock plateaus, Yaeju Dake on the left and Yuza Dake on the right. Two thousand yards apart, they were separated by a lower plateau. It rose in two escarpments until merging with the two converging hills over a thousand yards south. The 381st was to attack Yaeju Dake, known as the "Big Apple," while the 383rd was to take Yuza Dake, known by us as Hill 167.

Our supply situation was now very critical. After receiving a successful airdrop, we confined ourselves to patrolling and mopping up, using satchel charges to seal shut caves and flamethrowers to clean out pillboxes and foxholes.

On June 10th, the 2nd and 3rd Battalions began their attack on Hill 167. The 2nd found themselves under intense machine-gun fire from Yuza Ridge and from the hills to the west in the Marine sector. We pounded the enemy positions with every heavy weapon in the book, including the new 57-mm and 75-mm recoilless weapons. By nightfall, though, the Japanese were still firing. The 3rd, attempting to get on the lower escarpment to the left of Hill 167, also met heavy fire.

On the 11th, elements of the 3rd gained the first level. Despite infiltration attempts during the night, they were able to hold on. The 2nd, meanwhile, had a fight on their hands in the town of Yuza. They were still under fire from the guns of the day before and found themselves up against a nest of snipers. They killed about 15 Japanese, including an officer, but at dusk, they had to withdraw. Infiltration was heavy that night, and in the vicinity of Yuza, a large group of Japanese dressed in civilian clothes headed for our lines, pushing women and children ahead of them. In all, the 2nd killed 33 Japanese soldiers during the night.

On the 12th, elements of the 2nd again moved into the town of Yuza and again found it swarming with Japanese. They were very thick in the southwest corner, where they had a headquarters. After a day of close-in fighting, the 2nd had the town pretty well mopped up and established a perimeter on the southern edge. That was where we ran into our first serious trouble with antipersonnel mines, and two men were fatally injured.

Other elements of the 2nd established positions on the northern slope of Yuza Ridge. They took casualties from a reinforced pillbox, which the Japanese had abandoned but now occupied once again. Like the previous night, the Japanese seemed to be everywhere. The situation was thoroughly confusing because, while some were up to no good, others were civilians clutching surrender leaflets and obviously trying to surrender.

On June 13th, the 1st Battalion was committed and given the objective of seizing the town of Ozato and enveloping Hill 167 from the west. Company A reached a ridge 150 yards northwest of the town and sent a patrol to investigate the town. They encountered only civilians, but on the way back, their patrol leader, Sgt. Charles Thompson was killed by an antipersonnel mine, an ominous sign of what was to come.

Later in the day, A and B Companies drove to the southern edge of the town with no difficulty and then dug in for the night. About 5:30, while Capt. Van Vulpen, and Capt. Eric Newman, A Company Commander, planned their defenses, a member of the party tripped over a wire and detonated four or five mines planted halfway up an adjacent wall. The tremendous explosion virtually wiped out the party. Killed in the blast were Newman and four of their NCOs, while Capt. Van Vulpen sustained massive injuries. The only ones to escape were Capt. William Vallery, D Company Commander, and Pfc. Benjamin (Ben) Webster, who had been Capt. Van Vulpen's radioman. I think Ben was the one who couldn't get over it because he was the one who had tripped over the wire, triggering the explosion.

I talked with Capt. Van Vulpen while we were waiting for the jeep to carry him back to the hospital. Both his legs had been blown off, but he seemed unaware of the extent of his injuries because he was alert and talking to us. We were all in a state of shock, and he told us to carry on with the fight, that he would be okay. We received word later that Capt. Van Vulpen had died at the hospital. 1st Lt. William Griffith assumed temporary command of B Company.

Tragedy had again struck the 1st Battalion. Suffering heavily at Kakazu, they had been chewed to pieces trying to take Charlie and Love Hills. Now, in a single day, they had lost their battalion commander and every rifle company commander. To compound the situation, a few hours before this disaster in Ozato, Colonel Nelson and Capt. James L. Spratt, C Company Commander, had been wounded by mortar fire.

Col. Prosser Clark, wounded early in the campaign while commanding the 2nd Battalion, was just back from the hospital. He assumed command and reluctantly drew the companies back to the northern edge of the town. Numb from the shock of losing our men, we dug in there for the night, not knowing what to expect. I had come to know the three NCOs from our company very well: Sgt. Bertie Matney, Sgt. Albin Puhlaski and Sgt. William Wilson – as did everyone else in the company. Sgt. Wilson (Slim), a tall, blonde-haired young man, only a couple of years older than me, had been my squad leader in basic training.

The next day, Col. Clark sent patrols to work with the regimental anti-mine squad in the town. Unable to find all the mines, they still opened channels we could move through. Ozato had been the headquarters for a Japanese engineer unit, and it appeared that before pulling out, they had used up their supplies in laying their deadly trap.

On the 14th, for the second time in eight days, we again lost our regimental commander. While directing his troops from a forward observation post, an artillery shell wounded Col. Ballard, and Col. Williams of the 381st assumed command. On that day, we also received a new company commander, Capt.

Dorus C. Williams. The new commanders' situation was that Big Apple Hill was firmly under the control of the 381st, while Hill 167, with its approaches still heavily defended, remained in enemy hands.

June 15th, the 383rd attacked Hill 167 from two directions. The 1st Battalion was attacked from the west through Ozato. The 3rd, from their position to the east, was attacked from the lower slope.

Colonel Clark sent A and B Companies through the cleared portion of Ozato, and A Company got about 200 yards up the slope before they were pinned down by machine-gun fire from Hill 167 and the rear slope of Yuza Ridge. We were pulled back under cover of supporting artillery fire while a second attempt was made with all three companies. The 2nd Platoon of A Company made a rush toward the crest, but as they moved up the slope, their platoon leader was killed by machine-gun fire. Unable to overcome the resistance, we pulled back to just south of Ozato for the night.

On June 16th, the 3rd Battalion, 382nd, relieved the 1st Battalion, 383rd, in Ozato. We had been on the front lines since May 10th, and we were utterly exhausted and low in manpower. The 3rd Battalion, 383rd, had not been as hard hit as the other two battalions and was left on the line with the 382nd. While we were relieved from the front lines, we were still close to the units on the front lines. We did not go to a rest area but had to be ready to help if needed. The 3rd Battalion, 382nd, attacked the solid Japanese positions on the western slopes of Hill 167 but had no better luck than the day before.

Gen. Bradley, anxious to move south, ordered the 3rd to bypass the hill and move to the south.

The next day, the pocket of resistance on Hill 167 still needed to be dealt with, and the 1st Battalion, 382nd went to work on it from Yuza Ridge. They encountered mines of every description all day long, from artillery shells set in the ground with the fuses pointed up to tin cans set in the ground filled with explosives and scrap metal. Tanks were available, and they did a fine job cleaning out caves and pillboxes with flamethrowers. By the end of the day, the Battalion had moved about 800 yards. They had a line stretching from Ozato to a point about 300 yards short of the southwest corner of Hill 167.

The 382nd Anti-Tank Company moved to occupy Yuza Ridge that night. Cleaned out twice, the ridge was still swarming with Japanese. At least 20 were killed that night. It was later determined that a tunnel connected it with the pocket on Hill 167. The tunnel was at least 2,200 yards long.

The next day, June 18th, with the help of tanks, the 2nd Battalion moved up on the crest of Hill 167. They flushed out a considerable number of Japanese. The 2nd Battalion was now able to inflict tremendous damage on the fleeing enemy, accounting for about a hundred Japanese dead. Tanks supporting the 3rd Battalion, 383rd, located about 200 yards to the left of the 382nd, also bagged a considerable number of the enemy.

Although we did not know it at the time - and wouldn't know it until days later - General Buckner, commander of the 10th Army, was killed on June 18th while observing troops from the field. He was killed in action within the lines of the 381st Regiment of the 96th Division by enemy artillery on a hilly ridge in Okinawa.

On the 19th, the 96th Division suffered another loss. Brigadier General Claudius M. Easley, the lion-hearted little Texan who had been General Bradley's eyes and ears through both campaigns, was killed while at an infantry observation post on his daily tour of the front. His aide had been wounded first, and General Easley had quickly crawled to the crest of a small hill to direct fire on the gun. Easley was shot through the head by a Japanese machine gun and instantly killed. His death was a staggering blow to the Deadeyes of the 96th. General Bradley later called him the spark plug of the Division. Three weeks later, on July 12th, a monument was dedicated to him on the hillside where he was killed.

I remembered General Easley from my basic training days. We were on the rifle range at Camp White learning how to shoot Army style, and we were supposed to have a coach with us when we were on the firing line. When it was my turn on the line, we were preparing to fire, and I didn't have a coach. I called for a coach, and a person knelt beside me. When I completed my firing, the coach stood up and said, "Well done." When I looked up, I saw it was General Easley and his "BIG" one star.

Recognized in the military for his marksman abilities, he had developed the method of shooting for the U.S. Army. Because of him, we all became good shooters and were called "The Deadeyes."

[13] Members of the 96th Infantry on top of Yaeju Dake

---

[13] (US Military Archives, 1945)

[14] This is the last photograph taken of Lt. Gen. Simon B. Buckner, Jr., USA, right, just before he was killed on 18 June, observing the 8th Marines in action on Okinawa for the first time since the regiment entered the lines in the drive to the south. Note the rock and coral outcropping to his left. The shell that exploded hit that outcropping, dispersing fragments into the general, killing him within a few minutes. The other two staff officers were not seriously hurt.

---

[14](Rogers, Pfc. Frank C., Wikipedia Commons, 1945)

CHAPTER 9

The Enemy's Last Stand

Yaeju Dake and Yazu Dake

After we were relieved from active combat on the front lines, we were in Division Reserve. I do not recall that we ever saw duty on the front lines again. We kept moving up with the rest of the Division as they advanced, though, always at the ready. They continued to close in on the Japanese on the tip of the island, and the noose was tightening.

On the 20th, the town of Aragachi fell, and the G.I.'s of the Division swept on. Some of them were giving their commanders gray hairs because they were standing up, moving in a skirmish line, firing as they went. Eight Japanese trapped in a tomb threw out a half-dozen sabers, apparently in the vague hope that the G.I.'s would take the souvenirs and leave them alone, but the only thing they received was a satchel charge of explosives.

Civilians were increasingly becoming a problem, and various battalion intelligence sections had a wild night, herding hundreds of civilians to the rear. We were helping by guarding them as they were placed in compounds. They were the enemy, yet we couldn't help but feel compassion for these unfortunate people. In recent days, the distressing sight of dead and maimed women and children had become commonplace. Some were suicides, but many more were victims of the guns of our artillery. They took it all with stubborn stoicism; they had been kicked around all their lives, and this latest horror was just one more cross to bear.

I am writing this so that you, my children, and your children may know and understand what happened in my life during those two years of World War II. The next portion describes what I saw and expresses my feelings about what I saw on Okinawa. This is only about one town, but it was seen wherever we went.

An officer who entered Aragachi the morning after we had taken it wrote the following:

> "Aragachi was a living, stinking testimonial to the horror that war brings to a civilian population. The men who, of necessity, had laid it waste were Americans, and though they hated the Japanese soldier, they spared the natives whenever it would not endanger their own lives to do so. But the natives here had been caught, partly by the force of circumstance and partly by a fear of the advancing Americans, a fear bred of constant propaganda from the Japanese Army."

> "Consequently, they huddled in their holes, refusing to give up until burned or blasted out — some killing themselves and their children rather than face the horrors they had been led to expect. As morning came on [June] 21st, the town lay burned and broken under the hot sun with the sickly smell of death hanging like an unseen mist

over the rubble. Old men, women, and children dressed in tattered black kimonos were herded to the rear by the dozens. One had to walk carefully, for the dead were everywhere."

"Against the base of a stone wall was the naked body of an infant about a year old. No one seemed interested except the hundreds of flies that swarmed over it. There was little noise except for the occasional zing of a die-hard sniper's bullet and the distant chatter of machine guns. For Aragachi, the war was over. The little town had paid the price for the empire lust of the Tokyo warlords." [15]

General Bradley committed the 305th Regiment of the 77th Division to fight the last Japanese positions, Hills 79 and 85 south of Medeera, on the 21st. They met die-hard opposition but secured both hills by the afternoon of the 22nd.

The Japanese, although now pocketed, still held strong positions on the reverse slopes of Medeera Ridge and showed no tendency to let them go cheaply. However, individual soldiers had been showing an increasing willingness to surrender, and large numbers of civilians were trapped just ahead of our lines. On the morning of the 21st, Japanese/American interpreters were brought forward with

---

[15] (Davidson, Willems and Kahl; 1947; p188)

loudspeakers to broadcast a surrender appeal. Most such efforts in the past had resulted in increased mortar fire, but this time, the words of the interpreters brought results. So much so, that our forces had to twice postpone an attack as Japanese soldiers and civilians streamed into our lines. In all, 142 soldiers, many of them Korean labor troops, two nurses, and about 1,500 civilians surrendered to us that day.

At 10:30 that morning, our troops attacked the reverse slopes of the ridge. They were under constant sniper and machine-gun fire and found that one small knoll was completely hollowed out to form a fortress with six entrances. 25 Japanese soldiers and 6 officers were killed in this spot, and no estimate could be made of how many were sealed up inside. The infantry, with supporting tanks, flushed out another 50 from the many caves and crevices. That day was a day of violent action, and mopping-up exercises netted an amazing total of 1,347 Japanese known killed.

Our troops reconnoitered the town of Medeera on the 21st, and on the afternoon of the 22nd, the entire 3rd Battalion, 381st, attacked the town. It proved to be a block-by-block battle. Ten Japanese were killed in the first block, and in the second block, they fought a pitched battle with grenades. In the third block, the Japanese holed up in the high walls and hurled grenades by the dozens at our G.I.'s, each saving his last one to blow himself up. In the last of the ten blocks, a group of trapped Japanese officers fought furiously for a half-hour, then they, too, committed suicide.

The town was dotted with air-raid shelters, each filled with Japanese soldiers who had to be blasted out with grenades, flamethrowers, and satchel charges. By evening our troops were still fighting in the last block. Despite our advances of the day, there were still many Japanese soldiers in the town, so the battalion pulled back to the ridge for the night.

Officially, the battle was now over. On the night of the 21st, with the Japanese compressed into two or three scattered pockets, Lt. Gen. Roy S. Geiger of the Marines, who had assumed temporary command on General Buckner's death, radioed Admiral Nimitz that organized resistance had ceased. On the morning of the 22nd, the victory was celebrated in a flag-raising ceremony at Tenth Army Headquarters — to, what else — the strains of the Marine Hymn. *(I still say the Marines toot their own horn because no one else will!)*

It seemed the news of the victory celebration had not been given to the Japanese, and those in Medeera fought like madmen on the 23rd. The 2nd Battalion encountered the strongest position of this battle at the southern edge of the town. Two flame-throwing tanks were used but were unable to flush the Japanese out until a demolition team blew out a section of the wall with satchel charges. What followed would probably not have happened with any other enemy as 57 men were roasted by flame throwers in the courtyard, and many others were picked off trying to escape.

The 3rd Battalion, 383rd, beyond Medeera, had a brisk fight in a village on its outskirts and then came under fire from a wooded promontory. Calling up tanks and flamethrowers, they cleaned it out against stubborn resistance in a skirmish, which included wiping out a six-man machine gun nest and killing another Japanese soldier just in time to prevent him from satchel-charging one of the tanks.

On the 24th, the Japanese still would not quit. The 3rd Battalion encountered many one-man and two-man sentinel posts dug into rocky crags and ran into another massive cave in the southern part of the village they had worked over the day before. Late in the day it was determined that this cave was the headquarters of the Japanese 24th Division. A prisoner reported that the division commander, Lt. Gen. Tatsumi Amamiya, and about 200 troops were still inside with enough food to last thirty days.

Two days later, while the 96th Reconnaissance Troop stood guard, a detail from the 321st Engineers opened up the sealed cave so our loudspeakers could broadcast a surrender appeal. Undoubtedly, many of the soldiers would have been willing to give up, but General Amamiya had guards posted at strategic points to prevent anyone from escaping. All appeals failed, so 1,700 gallons of gasoline and 300 pounds of dynamite were brought up, and the cave was permanently sealed. On the same day, the Recons blasted a small cave nearby, which prisoners said had housed the headquarters of the 22nd Independent Battalion.

While all of this was happening, we could hear the loudspeakers still pleading with the Japanese soldiers and the Okinawan civilians to surrender. Many of them did, but a large number threw themselves over the cliffs on the tip of the island and onto the rocky beaches below.

The 96th, in conjunction with the other divisions, began a sweep back to the Yonabaru/Naha highway. The Japanese were flushed out by the hundreds as we combed the hills and valleys, and by the time the cleanup was completed on June 30th, it was estimated that another 3,400 Japanese had been annihilated.

For many of the rear echelon units, this period was the liveliest week of the campaign. Each night, hundreds of by-passed soldiers came out of hiding and tried to make their way north to the mountains. Such organizations as the Division and Division Artillery command posts found themselves right on the main line of the underground railroad, and many clerks, staff officers, and headquarters jeep drivers got a chance to put notches in their seldom-used firearms.

By July 1st, the job was done. The climactic battle of the Pacific War was over. The 96th Deadeyes had collided head-on with what seemed to be the very core of each Japanese position and had killed an estimated 37,763 of the island's defenders. But the price was high for us, too. As a division, we had lost 1,598 men killed, and 5,614 men were wounded. Of these, the 1st Battalion, 383rd, had 558 men killed, 1,688 men wounded, and 57 from Company B had been killed. I don't know how many men we had wounded, because some were wounded and came back, as I did, and some never came back.

With the loss of Okinawa, Japan had lost any hope she may have had of stemming the American tide. Already, the homeland lay burned and broken under the terrible blows of our airpower, and with this great close-in airbase and springboard for the invasion in our hands, what had gone before would be as a gentle breeze. On June 22nd, the rulers of

Japan knew they were beaten, and in mid-July, three weeks before the atomic bombs, they asked the Russian Government to mediate for peace. Our terms were simple: unconditional surrender!

[16] Civilians on Okinawa surrendering to US Soldiers. (AP Photo)

---

[16] (Associated Press 1945)

CHAPTER 10

Hurry Up and Wait

My Birthday Present

We set up our tents in the Medeera area and began the task of getting our weapons cleaned and in order again, getting new clothing and equipment, having our meals in the mess tent, and just relaxing. Sure, we had reveille in the morning, calisthenics, and some close-order drills to keep us in shape, and the companies organized baseball and softball teams.

For the time being, we were in a relaxing phase. I had become involved with the softball team, and in addition to playing third base, I was the manager. We developed a pretty good team and won the battalion championship. Word had come down about a point system to be used to ascertain when men would be eligible to go back to the States and, eventually, home. Our first man to go back was S/Sgt. Dominic Mondell, the supply sergeant. Before he left, I was informed by the company commander I would be the new supply sergeant, and I could start sewing on my sergeant stripes.

Sgt. Mondell briefed me on everything he could think of, but his mind was really on going home. However, we had received most of our new supplies and equipment, so basically, what was left to do was pack the equipment for the next move.

One day, Joe Spellazza and I got passes for the weekend. We caught rides on military vehicles and went north to the Yontan

Air Base. At mealtimes, we would find a mess hall and the cooks would let us eat with them. We went to the Air Base because we wanted to see the new B-29 bombers which had just been sent there.

They looked like they were two blocks long, and the wingspan was just about as wide. When we stood by the wheels we were dwarfed, they were so huge. We stood under the plane and looked up at the bomb bay doors, and they must have been twenty or thirty feet above us. We found a place to bunk that night, and the next day, we hitched our way back to the company area. It was just a relaxing time for us. *(We were a couple of real Midwest America hicks; we had never seen anything like these big planes.)*

After I became supply sergeant, I had a 3/4-ton truck and a driver for my use. One day, I received permission from the company commander to use the truck and go to the 3rd Battalion to check on Maro and Darold. My driver was "Pop" Kosel that day, and the two of us went, first to I Company and then to K Company, only to learn that both of my friends had been killed. This was a sad day for me.

("Maro Clyde Learned died April 4, 1945, at 19 years of age. Darold Delton Lidtke was also just 19 years old when he died on April 9, 1945. Both were born in Westbrook, MN, and are buried in Cottonwood County, Minnesota." —JWZ, 2004)

After we got back to the company, we received word that we would be going to Mindoro, in the Philippine Islands. The rumor was that we were going there to prepare ourselves for the invasion of Japan and that we were to be part of a fifteen-division invasion force. But first, we were to rest and rehabilitate for our next combat assignment.

We had loaded all our equipment and supplies on ships and were waiting at the harbor on Okinawa when we received word that a typhoon was coming. The men were ordered to board the ship, and our group of ships moved out to sea. The typhoon hit us late in the afternoon, and - boy! - did we have a wild ride!

Several of us who didn't get seasick decided we wanted to see what was going on, so we stayed up on top deck. The ship was rocking from side to side, plunging up and down from bow to aft, and sometimes trying to do both at the same time. It was tipping so far over, as it rocked, that I think we could have touched the waves by reaching over the rail. And the rain was so heavy and thick you could only see a few feet in front of you. We finally went below to our bunks, but I will never forget that wild ride.

The next morning, we could see the shores of Okinawa from our ship. We had gotten quite a distance from land before the typhoon hit, and now we were almost back to where we had started.

As we sailed toward the Philippines, the startling news of the atomic bomb, Russia's entry into the war, and Japan's peace offer bounced from ship to ship, all the way to Mindoro. We hadn't heard about Japan asking Russia to intervene and to act as an intermediary. It was three days later when they surrendered.

We landed on Mindoro, later known as "The Rock," on the 12th of August. One of the first things we received after we got into our assigned area was mail from home. My twentieth birthday was just three days away, and I had a card and letter from Mom wishing me a happy birthday. She wrote in her letter that she hadn't sent a present, but maybe I would get a better one later. How did she know?

Three days later, on August 15, 1945, my birthday, we got the word: Japan had surrendered! My Birthday PRESENT! It is celebrated here in the States on the 14th, but it was the 15th in the Philippines and Japan.

When we moved into our new area on Mindoro, my supply room was on top of a low hill in a long wooden frame building with metal siding part way up and then a section that was screened. A large canvas tent was over this with rolled-up sides that could be lowered over the screen in case of rain. One end held the company day roo,m and the other end was the supply room. My supply clerk/armorer and I also had space for our cots. I do not remember the name of the supply clerk at that time. I do remember he purchased a monkey, which he left when he went home. The monkey stayed as part of the supply room. Later, Eli Mandel became the supply clerk and armorer-artificer (the weapons maintenance man).

The company was in two rows of pyramidal tents over wooden frames with wooden floors. The company orderly room was in a building like the supply room and was across the end of the two rows of tents. An area about 50 feet wide was between the company tents and the supply room. This was where company formations and training sessions were held.

We were located less than a mile from the port city of San Jose. From our location, we could see the ships in the bay, and there was a lot of activity going on.

During the first weeks on Mindoro, our activities were pointed toward the expected occupation duty. Classes were started to teach the men the new duties of policing a defeated nation and a whole training program was put into motion along those lines. Spit-and-polish became the order of the day.

("It was a job trying to polish boots that had the rough side of the leather facing out, like suede, but we did it!" —JWZ, 2004)

While the whole world was in a happy commotion over the next few months, we sat like bumps on a log on this dull, unimportant island in the Philippines. The intermittent tropical rains seemed to wash away exciting rumors as they emerged. As the stay lengthened and nothing happened, the dry and dusty season set in to breed desolate boredom. And it didn't help the spit-and-polish either.

During this time, we were under the 24th Corps. We soon learned we were scheduled for occupation duty in Korea, but time dragged by, and we did not get any news about a departure date. When some news finally did break, it was the announcement that the move to Korea had been canceled. Almost immediately we were assigned to an occupation role in Japan itself, under the 6th Army.

Eager to leave Mindoro and see some of Japan while awaiting eligibility for discharge, we welcomed this news. As the ships assigned to carry the Division to Japan began anchoring in the bay, the 381st, assigned to leave first, began leveling their area. They tore down tents and burned and destroyed wooden kitchens and other buildings. They began policing up their areas, and some even boarded ships. Then, another change of plans filtered through, and the trip was off.

Division staff sought various means to alleviate the boredom caused by the situation. They eased off on routine training and set up an extensive program of education and athletics, while Special Services brought better movies and some USO shows to the island. These things made life bearable, but they did not quench our thirst for home.

Before long, the food began to improve, as did the movies, and even some beer started to come ashore. Each man in the company was authorized one case of beer a month, 24 bottles.

("Actually, the beer was better tasting than the water we had, but some men still did not drink it." —JWZ, 2004)

It was part of my job to requisition the beer and distribute it to the men of the company, so I guess, in addition to my other duties, I was also a bartender! I allowed myself one bottle of beer a day. We did not have any men abuse their beer ration, and go on a binge. The extra rations - from those who did not drink - were rationed out to those who wanted a few more bottles. Twenty-four bottles did not come out to a bottle a day per man.

I guess I should say here that some men will find a way to get hard liquor no matter where they are, and we had some do this. Of course, it was provided by the natives, and they didn't know where it came from. We had one man who became very ill after a night of drinking liquor that poisoned him. He made it through a stay in the hospital and lived to go home to Iowa.

The Red Cross, stationed on the island before we arrived, scattered its girls throughout the infantry and artillery, putting up large tents in those areas. Fatigue Junction, the Red Cross building in the town of San Jose, became a favorite place for the off-duty G.I.'s and offered such things as pocket billiards, ping pong, cards, bingo, cokes and cookies, and parties.

I went there a few times with Pop and Billy B. Richardson, another driver, just to get away from the boredom. One time there was a Filipino barber set up in front of the building. My hair needed to be cut, so I decided, "Why not?" He didn't have a clipper, just a comb, and a razor, so I got my first and only razor-cut haircut. He did a really good job, too.

The swimming pool in San Jose offered freshwater swimming to those who preferred it to the ocean. Swimming at the beach and bunk fatigue rounded out the day before evening chow and the usual night at the movies, or if you wanted, there was the inevitable poker game in one or more of the tents. With all of this, there was still the irritation about the mix-ups over shipping out for home, the point-score muddle, and movie projectors that broke down eight times a night. All these things tore at our patience and made "The Rock" a potential one-way ticket to an asylum.

It was about this time that the staff of the Deadeye Dispatch, the Division newspaper, decided they had to do something about the morale of the units. Someone, or several "someones," came up with the idea that the Division needed to have an "Occupation Girl," a pin-up girl. So, they started a contest to pick one. Anyone could nominate their favorite pin-up movie star. Little did they know what they were starting!

The contest started innocently enough. Names like Yvonne De Carlo, Betty Grable, Rita Hayworth, Linda Darnell, Olivia DeHaviland, Joan Leslie, and June Allyson were among the early contenders. Toward the end of the first week, however, a newcomer with no sex appeal or glamour, and fully clothed, popped up among the leaders and stirred up a commotion in the Division that didn't subside until she had the title tucked away in her lumberjacket.

"She" was Marjorie Main, the raucous, talkative, two-fisted, pistol-packing darling of the horse operas. The Division had seen her as Wallace Beery's heartthrob in the movie "Jackass Mail" on Okinawa just after the campaign ended. Fanned by the slogan "A Fighting Girl for a Fighting Division," her popularity whizzed through the Division, and before long she was in the lead.

Those who wanted a delicate brand of beauty tried in vain to stem the tide but were unsuccessful. The bored Division Band jumped on Marjorie's bandwagon and roamed the island whooping it up for her from trucks emblazoned with slogans — "Remember the Main," "As Main Goes So Goes the Division," and "Reminds Me of Mom." Today, she is perhaps best known as Ma Kettle from the Ma and Pa Kettle movies.

Even generals and colonels became volunteer workers on her behalf. When it was all over, Marjorie had six thousand votes, a thousand more than her closest competitor, Joan Leslie.

After the publicity about the contest was aired in the States, the Division became almost as famed for their eccentricity as for their valor. Miss Main said she was speechless and thrilled by her popularity among a group of famous soldiers, and she cabled her appreciation to the Deadeyes through General Bradley. She also forwarded two autographed photos, and promised to meet the Division — but not in a bathing suit — when it arrived back in the States.

From the Los Angeles Times story:

"A lusty, old-time western welcome greeted 1,800 men of the famed 96th (Deadeye) Division at the Los Angeles Port of Embarkation yesterday. The 1,800 men, among the 3,081 returning veterans arriving in the harbor aboard the transport General Langfitt, got a special greeting from Marjorie Main, the western pistol-packing motion-picture actress who was voted the "pinup girl" for the division in a spirited contest.

Miss Main, decked in a 10-gallon hat and with two guns at her hips, greeted the men from aboard the Port of Embarkation greeter ship Snafu Maru and then went aboard the General Langfitt. Later, she went to Camp Anza's staging area to help serve the division men their first Stateside dinner....

Miss Main was elected "Occupation Girl" of the 96th Division because her two-fisted screen characterizations embodied the same rugged virtues that carried the division through campaigns in Leyte and Okinawa."

# # #

Even before the war's end, the number one subject had become the all-consuming matter of discharge points. In the long weeks on Mindoro, the subject became an obsession with the homesick G.I.'s. When the long-awaited news finally came through that the 70-point men and the 85-point officers would sail for home, it stirred up only a slight display of enthusiasm. We had been hearing so many rumors that did not pan out that we wanted to see it before we would believe it.

(*"The discharge points were a system of a certain number of points for the time you'd been in service, and then you'd add points for the number of months you'd been overseas. So, the older men and the guys that had been in service the longest were going home first. Then we got low on men, so they merged three companies."* —JWZ, 2004)

About 2,300 men who were combat veterans of the Division's two operations were sent by LCIs to Mindanao, where they joined the 31st Division for eventual shipment to the States. At about the same time, 2,500 men from the 31st, the "Dixie Division," were moved to Mindoro to join the 96th in sweating out The Day. After the men going to Mindanao had left the Company, 1st Battalion Headquarters decided that since the companies were short of men, we would put three companies together.

Now, F and K Company came and joined us in B Company, and we all became Company B. The other two companies were disbanded, except on paper. And then A and E and I Companies merged with us, and that gave us enough men for a while. Then, I think it was the 31st Division that Shorty Madison was in, and they came. Some of their men came in, and they put them in our companies; that's how Shorty got into B Company. And guys were still leaving, too. But finally, as we were getting loaded up and ready to go, they decided we were going to go back to the States. The whole division – what was left of it – was going back.

In Company B, we received another supply sergeant from Company K, Sgt. Henry Snow, and his armorer-artificer, Pfc. DeWayne Schroeder. We also received armorer-artificers from the 31st Division.

Other men were integrated into our Company, but these men were assigned to the supply room and were the men I became friends with, even though some didn't stay long.

The Company Commander told Sgt. Snow and me that the man who had the date of rank (whoever was made sergeant first) would be the Supply Sergeant. My date of rank was one day before Hank's, but we didn't have that much to do, so it didn't make much difference. We all became pretty good friends, too.

The departure of the higher-point men perked up those of us who remained since it was an indication that the shipping tangle was unraveling and that maybe there was something to this point system after all. Special Services went to work, and they revived interest in the Division Bowl, an amphitheater that had been constructed soon after we arrived at Mindoro. They organized a series of stage shows featuring the Division swing band, brought in several USO shows, and got us some better movies.

With all the higher point men gone, we were short of NCOs in the Company. So, when the order came down that we would be needed for guard duty at the Bowl for one night while a USO troupe was here, both Hank and I agreed to serve as NCOs of the guard. There wasn't much to do, mainly post new guards every two hours and check on them a couple of times during their two-hour shift. I remember sitting on the edge of the stage, visiting with one of the guards for a time. The USO troupe was headlined by Aldo Ray, I think, or maybe Alan Hale Jr., now best known as the Skipper from "Gilligan's Island."

As time dragged by and we entered November, we were plunged into another form of service: policing the island. Our men found themselves busy day after day combing the rubble of war in our area and salvaging American equipment that was ready for shipment to the dumps on Luzon.

After a day of loading this equipment onto the ships, our men would come back to the Company area with their fatigue jackets off and the jackets would be filled with food the sailors on the ships had given them. I was the only one in the supply room who didn't go on these work details, and many nights during this time, Pete Petropoulos, the mess sergeant, would bring some cooking utensils from the kitchen, and we would have the steaks the men had brought back that day. Of course, Pete got to share in the food, too.

Early in December, the second group of Deadeyes bid us a joyous farewell as about 6,600 men on converted Liberty ships embarked for Leyte on the first leg of their journey to the States. 80% were veterans of combat with the Division, while the bulk of the remaining men were replacements received from the 31st Division. This shipment cleared our ranks of enlisted men who had been with the Division since its first days at Camp Adair, Oregon. Only about 2,000 officers and men who had fought in both campaigns were left. For them, it meant another Christmas under the tropical sun of the Philippines.

Because the part of the Division that remained was only a skeleton of what it had been, the infantry regiments and Division artillery were reorganized. The troops of each regiment were consolidated into one. The men remaining in our company became part of Service Company, 383rd. I don't remember if there were any other companies except Battalion Headquarters Company. Our company was now so small and young that I was the ranking NCO, so I was made the acting First Sergeant at twenty years old. I didn't have much to do as the First Sergeant, but we had to produce many daily reports.

When we became part of the Service Company, we had to move to another area, which meant all our tents had to be taken down and our equipment moved. I know some of the men were selling the wooden framework of their tents to the natives even when they knew the Army would probably remove them. I know I could have sold the supply tent monkey to several different natives, but I finally gave it to a young Filipino boy.

Shortly before Christmas, we got the word that another 1,800 men and officers would be traveling to the States under the flag of the 96th Division, which was now to be deactivated. They would sail for the U.S. in January. Hooray, we are finally going home! The remaining men would be reassigned to other units in the Philippines to await their turn to come home.

Now the pressure increased on the men to sign up for another six months and go on occupation duty in Japan. Those of us going home in January were not going to jump on this, but some of the other men decided that if they were going to stay over here even longer, they might as well see what Japan was like. I think they were offered a bonus if they stayed. I know some signed up because they didn't have a real home to go back to.

Even though Christmas was to be spent away from home, it turned out to be a happy one for those who would be eligible to accompany the Division home. The others could at least be thankful for peace, and most of them made the best of the situation. Special Services and the Red Cross girls did their best to make Christmas as joyous as possible. Each regiment and the artillery had parties at their individual Red Cross clubs, while Special Services put on an evening party at Fatigue Junction.

With officers serving as volunteer KPs and beer-jerkers, enough potatoes were peeled to make 200 pounds of French fries, 3,000 hamburgers were served, and 10,800 bottles of beer passed over the counter, all on the house.

On New Year's Eve, Special Services had the same kind of party at the 382nd Regiment's enlisted men's club. This time, the first three-graders volunteered to do all the work. Lucky me, I was only a buck sergeant, the fourth-grade, so I got the night off. Those guys prepared and served 4,500 hamburgers. 400 pounds of French fries, and 14,400 bottles of beer. *(Well, what else did you expect us to eat? After all, we are Americans!)* They also had coffee and Coca-Cola to drink since not everybody drinks beer, and I am sure some had strong liquor.

As we entered the new year, we still had to have morning formations and so forth, but nobody particularly cared. Once we got on board the ship, all the records and reports were turned over to Division Headquarters, and we were just soldiers on our way home—finally, going home!

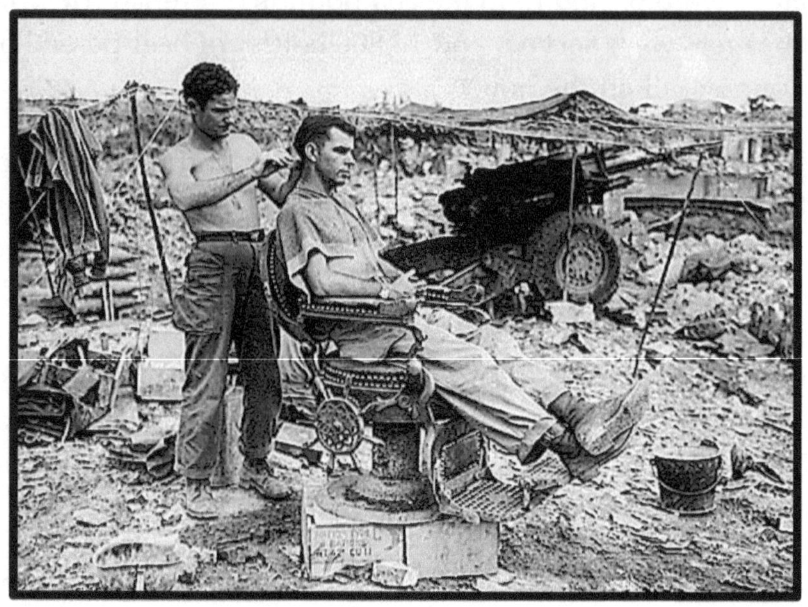

[17] Private First Class Troy Dixon, Leadhill, Arkansas, uses a Japanese barber chair to cut the hair of Sergeant John Anderson, Anita, Pennsylvania. Both men are members of the 363rd Field Artillery Battalion., located near Shuri. Okinawa, June 10, 1945.

---

[17] (U.S. National Archives Catalog, 10 June 1945)

[18] WELCOME HOME: Marjorie Main, the pistol-packing western actress voted "pin-up girl" of the 96th Division, is hoisted on the soldiers of the Deadeye troops as she welcomed Pacific battle veterans on their arrival yesterday at Los Angeles Harbor. (LA Times Archives Photo)

---

[18] (LA Times Photo Archives 1946)

[19] The baseball team on Medeera was called the Big Dealers. Here's Wes in his Big Dealers shirt.

---

[19] (J. W. Zimmerli, Private Collection; 1945)

[20] Pfc. Elias Mandel in 1944

[20] (Mandel, Elias, Pfc., Service Picture; Private Collection;1945)

[21] Pfc. Elias "Eli" Mandel in 2017, about a year before he passed away in 2018. Born 8 December 1919, in Bridgewater, McCook County, SD. Died 29 April 2018, in Tempe, Maricopa County, AZ. Buried in the National Memorial Cemetery of Arizona, Phoenix, Maricopa County, AZ. One of Wes's dear friends.

---

[21] (Mandel, Eli, Pfc., Private Collection; 2017)

CHAPTER 11

Finally Home

A New Life

On December 31st, the Division was officially relieved of its area command. After the holidays, men and officers who were not sailing with the Division began dribbling off the island to other organizations and stations in the Pacific. The bulk of the men went to the 86th Division on Luzon.

Until the bitter end, the Army played a game of ring-around-the-points with the Deadeyes, and it wasn't until just days before embarkation that the official home-going scores were announced. When the word finally came, it read: enlisted men, 48 points; officers, 68 points. This meant that a small group of 1,714 enlisted men and 104 officers would carry the banner of the 96th back to the States.

We were alerted for embarkation any time after January 15th, but after the many times our plans had been shifted and canceled, we were skeptical. It wasn't until General Bradley and five other officers took off for San Francisco that we allowed ourselves the blissful thought that home might be just over the horizon.

On the morning of January 17th, those of us sailing with the Division began loading aboard the General Langfitt, an 18,000-ton Army transport ship that had arrived from Manila with about 1,500 men already aboard. At 2 p.m., the ship weighed anchor and headed out into the Pacific, en route to San Francisco.

The first seven days of the trip, we had rough weather and there was considerable seasickness. After that, it was a calm and peaceful voyage. Four of us from B Company, Eli Mandel, Joe Spellazza, Loren Brower, and I, would get together up on deck each day to play cards and mess around, even if the weather wasn't very good. The second day, one of the guys came rushing up to where the rest of us were sitting, and excitedly told us he had seen Buster (Walter) Phillips; Buster later joined us on deck.

When he had been wounded, Buster had been shipped back to another island hospital. After leaving the hospital, he had been hopping from one replacement depot to another, trying to get back to our Company. Like us, he had boarded this ship for the trip home because he had enough points. We were happy to see him because he had been part of our platoon when we went to Hawaii.

After we had been at sea four days, a floating mine passed by our ship less than a hundred yards away. It wasn't noticed in the rough seas by the lookout until we had passed it. It was a menace to shipping, though, so the ship stopped and fired on it with a 50-caliber machine gun and a 3-inch gun and sank it. Also, during that first week, the captain of the ship announced over the PA system that his orders had been changed *(what else is new?)*, and we were now heading for Los Angeles instead of San Francisco.

We crossed the International Date Line during our "cruise" home and were all initiated into the Order of the Golden

Dragon. I don't remember that we had to do anything, but to show we had been there, we all received a certificate and a small billfold card to keep; just little souvenirs.

The Deadeyes came home to what the Los Angeles Herald-Express described as "the most tumultuous welcome" ever given to returning troops at the Los Angeles Harbor. And, true to her word, Marjorie Main was on hand to greet "her boys." The sight of her brought shouts of delight from the Deadeyes as she came alongside our ship in an Army greeter boat. She was decked out in a 10-gallon hat, white cowgirl outfit, and pistols and holsters borrowed from Wallace Beery. The Los Angeles Musicians Association Orchestra and an Army band accompanied her from the pier.

Miss Main was greeted by General Bradley and a committee of men from the Division Staff. She was escorted aboard the ship, where her enthusiastic followers hoisted her onto their shoulders with abandon. The newspaper reporters and photographers on hand for our return loved it. She proved herself a trouper worthy of the fighting men who had adopted her.

We all enjoyed the coffee, milk, and doughnuts the Red Cross ladies provided as we boarded the train to take us to Camp Anza, a desert camp about 60 miles east of Los Angeles. Miss Main rejoined us there and helped serve the steak dinner provided for all returning soldiers.

At Camp Anza, General Bradley was on hand to say his last word to us, "For you, this is one of the happiest days of your lives. For me, it is about the saddest. I won't say goodbye, because someday, somewhere, we'll meet again. I salute you, the finest men I have ever known, and I wish each of you the best of luck."

After that we were caught up in the whirlwind routine the Army had devised for transforming soldiers back into civilians. Staff personnel had been rushed from the Los Angeles docks to Anza by special transport and were busy grinding out final orders even before we arrived at the camp.

It was after dark on February 2nd when we finally arrived at the camp and were sent to barracks for the night. After we had eaten our steaks and settled into our barracks, Joe, Baldy, Loren, Buster, and I found the Post Exchange (PX), and each of us purchased a pint of ice cream, found a place to sit down, and ate the ice cream. Then we each got up, went and bought another pint, and, as we walked back to the barracks, we ate those. We hadn't had ice cream for almost a year and a half!

By noon on the 3rd, the first of the men were on their way to a separation center. That night, we boarded a train for our trip to Camp McCoy, Wisconsin. Joe would leave us in Kansas City to go to another separation center. I think we got to Camp McCoy on the 6th, and on the 7th, we made a brief run through the separation center assembly line. We were given physical examinations, turned in our old uniforms, and were issued new sets of khaki and olive drab uniforms and new boots. We kept our underwear and socks if they were in good condition. Seamstresses were on hand to sew on stripes and other insignias free of charge. We also kept our duffel bags to carry our clothing and other personal items home. Everything was rush, rush,

rush. We were also encouraged to join the Army Reserve, which I did before I was discharged.

On Friday, February 8, 1946, we received our pay, which included $300 mustering-out pay, received our discharge papers, picked up our travel orders and tickets, and boarded the train for home. The four of us were going by train to Mankato, Minnesota.

("All during this time, there were loudspeakers in the PX and everywhere, telling you what trains were leaving, and you would stop and listen and see if it was your train they were calling. It was about midnight when they finally called our train. And we boarded the train, and headed for Kansas City." —JWZ, 2004)

We got into Mankato early on the morning of the 9th. Brower and I left the train to catch the bus to Windom, Worthington, and Luverne in southwestern Minnesota. The bus depot was in a restaurant, so we had breakfast and then rode the bus to Windom, where I said goodbye to Loren and got off.

("He was going to Luverne, and I had to get off at Windom, so we went that way. And, I got into Windom, and it was on the ninth, and I called my folks. —JWZ, 2004)

The Windom bus depot was also in a restaurant, and I used the telephone to call my parents in Jackson, twenty miles south. They came up to get me and by early afternoon on Saturday, February 9, 1946, I was home with the family I loved.

(Somebody came and got me. I'm not sure if it was my dad. If it was, it must have been a Saturday, because otherwise, he'd have been working at that time of the day." —JWZ, 2004)

It was so good to be home. I was anxious to see the town, my family, and my friends. My brother, Dana, and my brother-in-law, Ray Mier, were already home from military service, as were several of my high school classmates.

I knew that on Saturday night, most of the family would be coming to my parents' house, so I borrowed my dad's car and went downtown. I visited stores where I knew people and went to the Motor Inn Garage to find Milton Wiehe, a high school friend. We went to Beech's Cafe for something to eat and to talk. Then I went to the J.C. Penney store to see Tony Lisko, the manager, and a friend. Tony wasn't in, so I visited with the pretty blonde young woman who was at the cashier's desk. I learned she had moved to Jackson with her family while I was gone, but she wouldn't tell me where she lived now, except that it was out in the country.

I guess I felt I didn't have any time to waste because I told her I would be back to take her home when she got off work. I ended up taking her and her sister home. Her sister had been the waitress I had seen at Beech's Cafe.

And that, my family, is when I met your mother and grandmother, with the pretty name (foreign-sounding to me), Dagny Synstelien. I was home, and a new life was beginning for me. Obviously, as it turned out, it was a new life for us.

# # #

I received several awards of medals and ribbons during my two years of service. To me, the most notable award was the Combat Infantry Badge, which I received twice, once for each campaign. As a result of being awarded this badge, I was also awarded the Bronze Star Medal. Also, I was awarded the Purple Heart Medal for wounds received in combat, the Good Conduct Medal, the American Defense Medal, the Asiatic-Pacific Campaign Medal (with two arrowheads for two amphibious landings), the World War II Victory Medal, the Philippine Liberation Medal (issued by the Philippine government), the Army Meritorious Unit Citation Ribbon, the Presidential Unit Citation Ribbon, and the Philippine Presidential Unit Citation Ribbon.

As you can see, I have a fair load of "fruit salad" to wear on my uniform. But as I said before, the Combat Infantry Badge is the one I am most proud to have earned. This was, and still is, a badge that all military personnel covet, even colonels and generals.

When I received my honorable discharge papers, I also received a certificate from the President of the United States, Harry S Truman, thanking me for my service in our country's armed forces. I am proud to have served my country in a time of war. Our hope and prayers were that we would never have to let our sons and daughters serve in another war. However, this has not been the reality.

We have had the Korean Police Action, the Vietnam War, the Persian Gulf War, the War in Iraq, and numerous other police actions. I pray that someday the leaders of all the countries of the world will see the futility of fighting, and sincerely seek peace in our world. Let us all pray this will happen!

— Jacob Wesley Zimmerli

[22] Wes and Dagny in October 1946, just before their marriage. They were married on October 20, 1946, to make the worst day of his life—the landing on Leyte on October 20, 1944—his best day.

---

[22] (J. W. Zimmerli , Private Collection1946)

Portion of an Interview

Partial transcript from an interview on March 15, 2004, with Adam Zimmerli (Wes's grandson).

"After coming home, I drove taxi for a year and five, six months, something like that, after I got married. When I first got home, I worked in a gas station, a service station. And I worked in that from April until the end of September. And we got married in October. The first of November, I started my own cab company. I had that until February of '48, from November of '46 to February of '48. And then your grand, your great-grandfather took that over in '48, and I went to work.

But I tried my hand at selling insulation for houses, and that went, it lasted a month or so. And then I went to work for a building contractor. And the whole summer of '48, I built steel Quonset buildings, or helped build them.

In the meantime, when I got out of the regular Army, I had signed up as a reservist, the Army Reserve, and I got my corporal's rank then, after I had already been a sergeant.

In May, April or May of '48, your uncle Carling asked me if I would join the Guard with him. The Guard already wanted me badly, because they needed a supply sergeant. So, I went into the National Guard as a staff sergeant. About November of '48, or October, November, somewhere in there, I went to work for the National Guard. And I worked for them as a unit caretaker.

I was the only maintenance caretaker. I took care of the vehicles; I was the supply, the vehicles, and stuff, in Jackson through December of '50. Well, actually, January fifteenth of '51, when the Guard was mobilized to go to Alabama for the Korean Conflict.

Then, I went to Alabama on active duty again. And I was supply sergeant there, and before I came home, I was first sergeant there. I got out of there in May of '52. On May 16, I was discharged and went to Jackson. Any World War II veterans did not have to go.

If they volunteered to go, they could go, and we did have a few guys that volunteered. But, most of us who were veterans did not go. (Our son) Paul was a child then.

So, then I came home from that one, and I went to work for a dairy, delivering milk. Carling worked there, and they needed another man, so I went to work for them, probably about the first of June, I suppose, because I came home in May. And, I worked for them until the following February, and then I went back to work for the National Guard.

This time, I had to go to St. James, where I was the unit administrator. We lived in St. James from '52 - I worked there and drove back and forth—from February until October. We built a house in St. James, and then I worked there until '56.

But I was going to say that at that time, I was a master sergeant. I wasn't a first sergeant anymore; I was a master sergeant. And I was a warrant officer. It must have been in '54 or '55 that I became a warrant officer. And then, in early '56, I got word that I didn't pass my physical. My heart was too bad.

And so, I went to a heart specialist in Mankato, and he told me, yeah, my heart was bad, and I better get out. So, I did. Then, after that, I got a waiver, notice of a waiver that I could've stayed in. But, I was already out.

In May, I started working in Jackson for Steiner Brother's Construction. I had put in applications at banks to try to get work in a bank so I could use accounting and do accounting. One of the guys in the bank at St. James was a friend of ours, and he had suggested I do that, as he had done that.

Anyhow, whatever I had, whenever I got out, I looked around for work and went here and there and everywhere. Even after I started in Jackson, I still made trips to various jobs.

But, Shorty Steiner knew us and asked if I wanted to work once when I was down in Jackson. I said sure. He said, well, I know you, and we need men, he said, and if the work's too hard, let me know, and you can sit down. Well, I went to work for him, I think, about the first of May, and Dagny stayed in St. James with the kids and sold the house. I think they moved … we moved them in June or someplace along in there and moved back to Jackson. I worked for Steiner Brothers for five years.

In the meantime, I went back to vocational rehab for veterans and took some accounting courses. While I was still taking some of those, I got a call to go to for an interview. I had to take a civil service test for accounting for the Welfare system in Minnesota. So, I went and took that, and then I got a call from Redwood Falls wanting me to come for an interview. I was accepted when I went for the interview, and I started working there in April of '61.

ADAM: In general, I guess, how would you say that your service, experiences during the war affected the rest of your life?

JACOB: Well, I think we had to grow up fast in the service, especially during wartime. I noticed this difference when I came back. The guys that I'd been to school with, my same grade in high school, that had not gone to the service. They'd maybe gone on to school, some of them, but they were still doing childish things, immature things. They hadn't grown up as much. They hadn't gone through what most of us who had been in the service had. So, it was an altogether different ballgame for them. And, maybe it made us appreciate a little more what we had here already, what we could see in other countries and other places. Of course, I got back into the military for another eight years. And, that made a lot of difference to me."

[23] Wes in 2019, living in The Homestead Assisted Living in Chariton, Iowa.

---

[23] (M. Zimmerli, Dad in The Homestead, Private Collection; 2019)

[24] Wes and Dagny on vacation in 2008 in St. Marys, GA

---

[24] (M. Zimmerli, Mom and Dad in St. Marys; Private Collection. 2008)

My Faith Journey

Written in 2012 and read 12/26/2018 at her funeral

I would rather call my testimony "my faith journey," because it has been a journey, one that has taken almost 86 years. And in many ways, it has been like a road trip, where you come to a sign that says, "Road Under Construction." Or perhaps it says, "Flagman Ahead," and you are stopped for a while, and then a vehicle appears with a sign on top that says, "Follow me," which you do, trusting that He can lead you up and down hills and around curves where you can't see ahead. Then you come to where the road is clear again and you can travel along without trouble until you come to another road construction sign.

I was very young during the Depression era, one of eight children. My parents belonged to the Norwegian Lutheran Church, so I went through Catechism classes and was confirmed. In that culture, religion was not a subject that came up in casual conversation, but my dad was the Sunday School superintendent, and he always gave good talks on how to live the Christian life, but personal salvation wasn't spoken of in family conversation.

When I was 14, I attended Bible Camp for a week. On Saturday night, there was a special revival-type service with an altar call. In my heart, I knew I was supposed to go forward, but

I was afraid if I did that, I would have to become a missionary, and I didn't want to leave the security of home. So, for many years, I felt like there was something missing, and I would have to live the best life I could in hopes of making it to heaven.

Many times over the years there were circumstances that had an impact on my faith journey. In early January 1958, my dad died unexpectedly, and a week later, I had to have a five-and-a-half-hour-long surgery. Eight days later, when I was discharged from the hospital, my husband was laid off from his construction job for the winter. Unemployment benefits had just become available, and with four sons and a wife to feed, he received $37 a week. We had begun to tithe at church before that, but I told him we just couldn't do it with so little coming and so much going. But he persisted, and $3.70 went into the offering plate.

Another instance was in May 1963. Wes' older brother had suffered a heart attack, and a couple of weeks later, his younger brother was burned to death in a propane tanker accident. I was pregnant with our sixth child, and one night, about ten days before he was due to be born, he died. The doctor said I had to carry him until he came naturally.

What a sad time. I carried him the full 10 days, and at last, he arrived, stillborn. I became very ill with what was then called childbed fever, though they know it is a form of sepsis today. I suffered a clinical depression that lasted a year and a half. It was a hard time for Wes and our other five sons. It felt as though my prayers just couldn't reach God, and I didn't understand what was happening.

Several years later, the really exciting part of my journey happened. One weekend, a group of people came to our church for a Lay Witness Mission weekend. There was a lot of praise-singing and personal sharing by the laypeople who had come to our church as part of the mission team and who had all been touched by Jesus. My tears flowed freely that weekend, and on Sunday morning, when the altar call was given, I knew I had to go up. It was so hard because my first thought was, "I'm president of the Women's Society, and supposedly a Christian. What will the people think of me if I go forward now?" When I knelt at the altar, I seemed to hear God saying to me, "Do you really mean business this time?" And I said, "Yes, Lord."

As the days went by, I didn't think I felt any different, but suddenly, I realized the God-shaped hole that had been in my heart was now filled. I had gained the assurance that Jesus had really died for ME and that I would go to heaven when I died. Even though I was very familiar with the Bible, I began to develop a thirst to read and read and read from it. Often, I would think, "God, when did You put _that_ in the Bible?" as the verses began to take on new meaning and importance.

The morning after the Lay Witness Weekend, I went to my office job and knew I had to witness to my co-worker, something I had never done before, and I was shaking all over. But I had read that the Lord would put the words in my mouth and He did.

As time went on, I found so many people who needed to hear that Jesus was still alive, and it kept getting easier. Wes and I began to pray together during our family devotions, talking to

God and each other about our problems and what concerned us. All these years later, we continue to do that each morning.

When I was growing up, one thing I never heard much about was the Holy Spirit, Who was only mentioned in the Apostles Creed as the Holy Ghost, both in my old childhood Norwegian Lutheran Church and in the Methodist Church that I joined in 1946 when I married Wes. (By the way, next Saturday we will have been married 66 years.)

In 1974, because of Wes' job, we moved forty miles away from our home in Redwood Falls, where we had lived for twelve years, to Marshall, MN. There, we found a very alive community-wide Christian group called the Full Gospel Business Men's Fellowship, International. We attended several meetings and found that the Holy Spirit is alive and well and plays a very important part in our lives. He is living right inside us, as close as our very breath. This group was also teaching that healings still take place today and did not stop with the Apostles of old, as some say.

We continued to attend the United Methodist Church and, for fifteen years, tried to share what God had shown us. We also joined the Lay Witness Ministry and, for 12 years, traveled all around the Midwest on weekends, giving our testimonies and enjoying a great time of growing in the Lord. Within our own church, we led small groups and began a home Bible study that continues to this day, about 27 years later.

[In 2011,] our faith got a real workout when we sold our home in Northern Minnesota while we were buying our new home in Chariton, IA, taking care of all the details ourselves. We ran up against many roadblocks, but God was so faithful. When we gave it all over to Him and were quiet before Him, He led us one step at a time and gave us His peace that does pass all understanding.

I haven't seen the "End of Road Construction" sign yet, so my faith journey isn't over. I am still amazed at how God will lead if you let him. He has much more in store for you than you can ever ask or even imagine.

So, thank you, Jesus, for touching me and leading me. I pray this humble message will have meaning for someone who is searching. God is the answer!

Wes's good friend for many years, Bill Koenecke, passed away in 1991. Bill was Wes's platoon sergeant starting out in 1945.

Final Notes

Wes and Dagny were married for 72 years. In 1961, they moved from Jackson, MN, to Redwood Falls, MN, where they lived until 1974. In August of 1974, they moved to Marshall, MN, for Wes's job. They lived in Marshall until 1989, when they retired and moved north to Little Bass Lake near Cohasset, MN. In 2011, they moved to Chariton, IA, a small rural town in the southern part of the state, for "one more adventure." Dagny passed in her sleep in the early morning hours of December 22, 2018, only a week before her 92nd birthday.

After Dagny's passing, Wes continued to live in The Homestead, Assisted Living in Chariton. His health began to decline in late 2023, and hospice was called in to help with day-to-day tasks. By early 2024, the decision was made to move him to a nursing home nearby. Wes moved into Southern Hills Specialty Care nursing home in Osceola, IA, on February 1, 2024, and passed away in his sleep on February 19, 2024, at age 98. A memorial service was held on June 8, 2024, in Redwood Falls, MN, where the ashes of Wes and Dagny were interred very near the grave of their stillborn baby boy, Mark Robert.

Wes and Dagny had five sons: Paul Wesley, Gary David, Kevin Eric, Michael Kent, and Brian Keith. A sixth boy, Mark Robert, was stillborn in 1963 in Redwood Falls, MN. Paul, the oldest son, was born in 1947 and died in 2017 in Wichita Falls,

TX. Paul had a long career as a journalist in the United States Air Force.

Gary has lived most of his adult life in the Mankato, MN, area. He was employed as a windshield glass specialist with several firms.

Kevin lives near Omaha, NE, where he was last stationed in a long career as a computer programmer in the Air Force.

Michael lives in coastal southeast Georgia. Michael was in full-time ministry for nearly seventeen years after moving to Georgia and is now a freelance writer, editor, and proofreader.

Brian has been a teacher, administrator, and coach in the Chariton, IA, school system for more than thirty years.

Personal Note From The Editor

The Spirit of the Deadeye division is still alive and well even though almost all the Deadeyes who fought in WWII are now deceased. That Spirit is kept alive primarily by their children, grandchildren, and other relatives. A wealth of information for offspring, relatives, and other interested persons is the Remember the Deadeyes website, located at www.rememberthedeadeyes.com.

The site contains updates on reunions, military records, back issues of the Deadeye Dispatch, and copies of the books and stories written by and about members of the Deadeye Division.

Another source of communication and education is the Deadeyes Facebook page. One Deadeye's son posted the following on Facebook in 2017 about Lt. General Buckner.

> *"I am posting tonight to remember Lt. General Buckner as a brave officer that led his men from the field. My father was in the line the day Gen. Buckner was killed. He recalled that day to me as it was etched in his memory one day in 2007. My father recalled to me that they had been pushing on the enemy for several days and there was a brief lull in the action. Troops were taking a brief rest with water and cigarettes when the General's jeep with his driver at the wheel passed along the road. Less than 100 yards from my father, a single*

artillery round was fired and dropped dead center of the General's jeep, killing him and the driver instantly.

The word passed quickly along the line from soldier to soldier that General Buckner was dead. The men were deeply hurt as they saw him as one of them, a 'foot' soldier. General Buckner has a small monument in Okinawa near where he was killed, and the Bay below the ridge was named Buckner Bay in his memory by the invasion force.

General Buckner was the son of Confederate General Simon Bolivar Buckner, Sr., who was also a Governor of Kentucky in the 1890s. My father always spoke of the respect and honor the men of the 96th infantry had for Lt. General Buckner, he was a leader of his troops to the end."

The Facebook site is often full of posts from people who say their father/grandfather/uncle, etc. never told them anything about their time in service. Members of the site and of the Remember the Deadeyes website point them to stories, documents, and books such as this one. On occasion, some have called Wes – notably the cousin of Maro Learned who had never heard any of the stories about Wes and Maro's early days in the US Army.

The Facebook site also has pictures, rosters, and communications from home to soldiers and from soldiers in the field back home to their family and loved ones. It is a useful tool for putting names and faces together, and passing along information about reunions and gatherings of the few remaining Deadeyes. Sadly, these days it is also useful for sharing in the passing of yet another Deadeye.

Now, you hopefully know more than you did about WWII and the Pacific Theater and what our young men – many not yet 20 years old – went through to preserve the freedoms we enjoy today.

Thank you for reading *One Soldier's Story*. Leave us a review where you purchased it or at amazon.com or goodreads.com. And tell your friends.

—Michael Zimmerli, ed.

To report typos or just to let me/us know how you liked the book, you can email me at mike@zimmac.com

About the Author

For the last thirteen years of his life, from 2011 to 2024, Jacob Wesley Zimmerli lived in southern Iowa. Whenever he left the house (or his room after moving into assisted living), he always made sure to grab his WWII/KOREAN WAR VETERAN cap.

One Soldier's Story was published in May 2021. A number of newspaper articles about his book and becoming an author at 96 followed, and KCCI-TV in Des Moines featured him on Veterans Day that year. He always said he was not a hero; he was just doing a job he was asked to do. Of the small group of young 18- and 19-year-old men from southern Minnesota who enlisted and trained with him, and were beside him in combat, he was the last survivor.

Jacob Wesley Zimmerli passed away peacefully early in the morning on February 19, 2024, at 98 years of age. He always liked getting an early start on a journey.

The picture Wes sent home to his mother
from Basic Training.[25]

---

[25] J. W. Zimmerli, Private Collection; 1944

SOURCES

Angell, Lowell. 2017. "Theaters in Hawaii have a Long and Colorful History." *StarAdvertiser*. January 15. Accessed April 2021, 23.

Archives, National. 1945. *National Archives*. June 14. Accessed April 16, 2021. https://commons.wikimedia.org/wiki/File:111-SC-337969_-_Riflemen_of_the_2nd_Bn.,_381st_Regiment_of_the_Tenth_Army%27s_96th_Div._peer_cautiously_ahead_as_they_advance_across_the_summit_of_Yaeju-Dake_escarpment_(Big_Apple_Ridge)_on_Okinawa._14_June_1945.jpg.

Archives, U.S. National. 1945. "American sniper with M1 carbine in cave on Okinawa." *Wikimedia Commons*. May. Accessed April 20, 2021. https://upload.wikimedia.org/wikipedia/commons/f/fb/Silhouetted_against_the_entrance_to_one_of_the_caves_that_honeycomb_the_Okinawa_hills%2C_a_Marine_rifleman_resorts_to..._-_NARA_-_532558.tif.

—. 1945. "U.S. National Archives Catalog." *U.S. National Archives Catalog*. June 10. Accessed April 16, 2021. https://catalog.archives.gov/id/531303.

Army, US. 1945. *Wikimedia Commons*. May. Accessed May 6, 2021. https://en.wikipedia.org/wiki/Battle_of_Okinawa#/media/File:Attack_on_bloody_ridge.jpg.

Davidson, Orlando R., J. Carl Willems, and Joseph A. Kahl. 1947. *The Deadeyes: The Story of the 96th Infantry Division*. Infantry Journal Press.

Flagg, James Montgomery. ca. 1917. "I want you for U.S. Army: nearest recruiting station." *Library of Congress*. Accessed April 2021. https://www.loc.gov/item/96507165/.

Hasselmann, Lynne. 2019. "Veterans Day 2019: Remembering Oregon's 96th Infantry Division." *OregonLIVE*. The Oregonian|OregonLIVE. November 10. Accessed April 2021. https://www.oregonlive.com/history/2019/11/veterans-day-2019-remembering-oregons-96th-infantry-division.html.

Hill, William R. n.d. *In Honor of Maj. Gen. James L. Bradley*. Accessed April 21, 2021. http://www.rememberthedeadeyes.com/GeneralBradley.html.

Koenecke, Kenneth W. ca 1944. "SSgt. Bill Koenecke." Private Collection. Used by Permission.

1946. *LA Times Photo Archives*. Accessed April 20, 2021. https://dl.library.ucla.edu/islandora/object/edu.ucla.library.specialCollections.latimes:3402.

Land, Pfc. Williams. 1945. "Only 12 But They Lick 150 Japs, Stars and Stripes Archives." *Stars and Stripes*. May 15. Accessed April 21, 2021.

https://www.stripes.com/news/special-reports/world-war-ii-the-final-chapter/wwii-victory-in-japan/only-12-but-they-lick-150-japs-1.359090.

Learned, Maro Clyde. 1944. "Pfc. Maro Clyde Learned." Private Collection. Used by Permission.

Mandel, Elias. 2017. "Pfc. Eli Mandel." Private collection. Used by permission.

—. 1944. "Service Picture."

Office, U.S. Government Printing. 1942. "Government & Geographic Information Collection." *Northwestern University Libraries.* Accessed April 21, 2021. https://dc.library.northwestern.edu/items/c7aa31e9-cd11-48b1-bd81-387f9afa762a.

Press, Associated. 1945. *Cleveland Marine recalls fight for Okinawa, last major battle of World War II.* Accessed May 11, 2021. https://www.cleveland.com/resizer/Qd4OjJXBdArYSA_wnLLRmdyEaN8=/1280x0/smart/advancelocal-adapter-image-uploads.s3.amazonaws.com/expo.advance.net/img/b8df484a6d/width2048/10c_civilians.jpeg.

Rogers, Pfc. Frank C. 1945. "Wikipedia." *Wikipedia Commons.* June 18. Accessed May 10, 2021. https://upload.wikimedia.org/wikipedia/commons/f/f4/Last_picture_of_LtGen._Buckner_at_Okinawa.jpg.

U, S, Military. 1945. "Military Archives." *WikiMedia Commons.* june 18. Accessed May 6, 2021. https://commons.wikimedia.org/wiki/File:On_top_of_Yaeju-Dake.jpg.

Zimmerli, Jacob Wesley. 1946. Jackson, MN, October.

—. 1944. "Love, Wes."

—. 1944. "One Raw Recruit." Jackson, Minnesota, February.

—. 1945. "The Big Dealer."

Zimmerli, Michael. 2019. "Dad in The Homestead." Chariton, Iowa, October.

—. 2008. "Mom and Dad in St. Marys." St. Marys, GA, November.

www.ingramcontent.com/pod-product-compliance
Lightning Source LLC
Chambersburg PA
CBHW021957120726
47992CB00001B/299